Literary Feasts

EXTRAORDINARY MOTIVATION
IN ENGLISH AWARD

Presented to

SAITHA WILS

by the Acton-Boxborough Regional High School
English Department
May 7, 2014

Literary Feasts

Recipes from the Classics of Literature

Barbara Scrafford

iUniverse, Inc.
New York Lincoln Shanghai

Literary Feasts
Recipes from the Classics of Literature

Copyright © 2005 by Barbara Lynne Scrafford

iUniverse books may be ordered through booksellers or by contacting:

iUniverse
2021 Pine Lake Road, Suite 100
Lincoln, NE 68512
www.iuniverse.com
1-800-Authors (1-800-288-4677)

ISBN: 0-595-32951-9

Printed in the United States of America

Dedicated to Uncle Jimmy, from whom

I first learned the pleasures of the table.

Contents

INTRODUCTION

I can think of no better way to spend an afternoon than lying on the sofa, eating bonbons and reading a novel. Transported to another world, I smell Willa Cather's new mown fields, the cheap perfume of García Márquez's Caribbean bordello, taste the smokey sweetness of Carson McCullers' black-eyed peas and rice. I have salivated my way through Virginia Woolf, Saul Bellow, Mark Twain, and so many others. I even craved canned spaghetti during Hemingway's *Big Two-Hearted River*. Who, I ask you, could resist Mrs. Ramsay's lyrical description of the *boeuf en daube* in *To the Lighthouse,* or Hemingway's glowing descriptions of food and drink in the down and out Paris of between the wars? Who, indeed, could read Flaubert's exuberant rendering of Emma Bovary's wedding feast of Normandy specialties without wondering what's for dinner tonight? Has anyone ever read *Through the Lookinglass* without being curious about "frumenty," or sympathized with the pathetic little inmates of Lowood Academy, Jane Eyre's alma mater, without imagining an oatcake?

We crave the victuals of a favorite heroine or hero just as we long to touch the ground where cherished books are set—to walk the shores of Walden Pond, the ebullient London streets of Dickens, to repeat the voyage of Odysseus, to dip a toe—just once—in the Mississippi mud. Such a visit enlarges the reading experience, and it makes it more a part of our own lives. When one has seen the sights, smelled the smells, and tasted the food, the book comes to life in our own sensory perceptions.

And so it was this desire—to know more fully my favorite books—that I came to write *Literary Feasts*. I have tried to make the recipes as accurate to the time and place of each novel as possible, and so some of the dishes are also suited in flavor, texture, and acceptable fat content to other times. Seasoning in the past was not always as subtle as it is today; much of what used to be steamed instead of baked, such as Jane Austen's apple dumplings, is downright soggy, especially with melted butter added to the finish. And some dishes are surprisingly bland, as in the epic "sancocho," so enthusiastically described by Gabriel García Márquez, which turns out to be nothing more than a boiled dinner, using the starchy yucca and plantain native to South America in place of the root vegetables of New England. Some dishes mentioned may not have existed at all, such as in John Steinbeck's *Cannery Row*, when Doc Rickets orders himself a beer milkshake at a local diner.

Although I have endeavored to be authentic, such an attempt is bound to result in an approximation. While most of the recipes stem from historical cookery books, the particular character a certain place or individual cook gives to a dish will be missing in this book except, perhaps, when the text gives clues, such as Mrs. Ramsay's reference to the yellow color of her *boeuf en daube*, which indicates the use of a white instead of red wine in the sauce.

Older recipes are usually quite vague as to amounts and procedures, so I simply assembled the ingredients and made the dish several times, adjusting the amounts as I went until I got something palatable that might have been what the author had in mind.

In general, the ingredients were readily available. A short search brought up the Gulf mullets of Kate Chopin's *The Awakening*; yucca and plantain abound in Hispanic markets, but the nettles for Levin's soup in *Anna Karenina* were a tough assignment. After a frustrating search, I finally found some growing wild in one of the municipal parks and did the city the favor, with the gardener's permission, of weeding one of its gardens of the pesky invaders. If you have a similar source, be sure to wash the nettles thoroughly, wearing rubber gloves, because as your Girl Scout leader warned you, they do sting the flesh.

I would like to thank my husband for serving as chief tester, for having the patience to eat clam chowder for a week as I worked on *Moby Dick* and steamed apple dumplings even once as I strove to get closer to the culinary center of Jane Austen's *Emma*, and for his always gracious research assistance, editing suggestions, and spelling corrections.

I hope *Literary Feasts* enriches your reading as much as the writing of it has enriched mine. It is said that you cannot truly know a man until you have walked in his shoes. I like to think that you also know a character better when you have tasted his food.

THE ADVENTURES OF TOM SAWYER

by
Mark Twain

Americans, with their nostalgic idealism for childhood, often hold up Mark Twain's classic *The Adventures of Tom Sawyer* as a model of innocent youth that no longer prevails in society, even though the story involves the eviscerating of cats, the carrying around of dead rats, parental negligence, and murder. The book is an episodic construction of children's pranks—the crazing of the cat with "painkiller," the snatching of the school-master's wig—which gets progressively more complex and dark as the story continues, with the midnight witnessing of a murder and the night spent in the cave with the evil Injun Joe, who in the end gets himself forever trapped and must resort to eating bats to keep from starving.

As is typical of Mark Twain's work, societal institutions—church, school, the legal system—come out a poor second to the purer world of children. At their best, the adults are kindhearted dupes. Aunt Polly is prey to purveyors of patent medicine and is the fool of her nephew Tom. And Widow Douglas actually thinks she can civilize that free-spirited rascal Huckleberry Finn. At their worst, the adults are, like Injun Joe, murderous, vengeful creatures of the night who prey upon anyone who happens to get in their way. Sometimes the only refuge a child has in such a world is his imagination.

Set between the innocent and simple pranks of childhood and the dangers of adult misbehavior is the idyllic Jackson's Island incident, when Tom, his best friend Joe Harper, and the town rapscallion Huckleberry Finn run away

1

from home. Brokenhearted in love, falsely accused of swiping the kitchen cream, and in the case of Huck, eager to escape the privations of society, the boys flee the adult world to create their own idyllic universe. The ensuing chapters form a lyrical paean to nature and childhood.

When they discuss what fantasies to pursue in their projected new life on Jackson's Island, Joe Harper favors pretending to be hermits, wearing sackcloth and ashes, eating only crusts of bread, and renouncing the world to dwell in the wilderness until they are taken by starvation, but instead they choose to play at pirates, with its action, camaraderie, and satisfying meals.

When the boys meet at the appointed place at the appointed hour—midnight, they have transformed themselves into outlaws of the seas.

> "Who goes there?"
> "Tom Sawyer, the Black Avenger of the Spanish Main. Name your names."
> "Huck Finn, the Red-Handed, and Joe Harper, the Terror of the Seas."

As befits thieves and marauders, they steal the provisions for their illicit camping trip to the island, for the true outlaw must in all ways reject the values of civilization. The Black Avenger, the Red-Handed, and the Terror of the Seas load contraband bacon, corn meal, and a skillet—all they need for a fine southern feast, onto a small raft and ride it downstream to the island. For several days, they are free of the stifling adult world and play out their mutual fantasy: exploring the island, watching the insects, listening to birdsong and frolicking naked in the river. In these precious stolen moments they hunt turtle eggs, feast on bacon and corn pone, fresh-caught catfish, and sleep contentedly, full bellied, beside the fire or in the warm sun. They are astonished at how good fish fried with bacon is. They had not known that cooking a fish immediately upon catching it is the best possible eating, and that fresh air and exercise vastly improve the flavor of any food.

They build their cooking fire just inside the forest and are delighted to be in what they imagine to be virgin territory, untouched and unsullied by the hand of civilization. They swear never to return to the society that has so wronged them.

"The climbing fire lit up their faces and threw its ruddy glare upon the pillared tree trunks of their forest temple, and upon the varnished foliage and festooned vines. When the last crisp slice of bacon was gone, and the last allowance of corn pone devoured, the boys stretched themselves out on the grass, filled with contentment. They could have found a cooler place, but they would not deny themselves such a romantic feature as the roasting campfire."

Throughout the book, Twain challenges the common notion that bread honorably earned is sweeter than ill-gotten gain. One of Tom's most infamous pranks, which occurs early in the novel, is built around the whitewashing of Aunt Polly's fence, which she has assigned him to do on a Saturday morning as a punishment for pilfering jam. Tom soon learns how to dupe the other boys into doing the job for him, and by the middle of the afternoon the fence has three coats of bright whitewash. Aunt Polly is impressed by Tom's ability to work hard and gives him a choice apple, along with a lecture on the added flavor a treat has when it comes through virtuous effort. Before she finishes, however, he has already stolen a doughnut from her kitchen.

Although stealing sweets such as jam and doughnuts is almost a way of life for Tom, he does suffer pangs of conscience for the plunder of the food that warms his belly on the island retreat. The stealing of ham and bacon, he decides, is far more serious than "hooking" such frivolous treats as doughnuts. Still, nothing has ever tasted better to him than this stolen feast in this stolen time.

000

CORN PONE

Corn pone, bacon, and catfish make a heavenly meal, especially when cooked over a campfire. Corn pone is a traditional bread of the Algonquin tribe, and common in the South. The longer the batter sits, the easier it is to form into "pones."

2	cups cornmeal
½	cup milk
1	teaspoon baking powder
1	cup boiling water
½	teaspoon salt
5	tablespoons bacon fat

Mix the dry ingredients together in a large bowl. Stir in the milk; then add the boiling water, 1/4 cup at a time. Let the mixture sit at least 10 minutes after the addition of each 1/4 cup of water, and check its consistency. The batter should hold its shape when formed into a vaguely cylindrical shape about the length of the palm of your hand. You may not need all of the water to achieve this. Stir in 3 tablespoons of the bacon fat. At this point the batter can be refrigerated for future use for as long as several days. When ready to cook, heat the rest of the bacon fat in a heavy skillet until it is very hot—barely smoking, then drop a few pones into the fat and fry on both sides until golden. Serve hot.
Yield: 8 pones.

FRESH-KILLED CATFISH

The boys are right. Almost nothing in this world tastes as good as a fish put in the frying pan just minutes after being caught. Covered with a cornmeal crust and served with bacon and corn pone, it's one of the best meals possible.

2	catfish
6 to 8	strips of bacon
2	cups of cornmeal

Unlike most other freshwater fish, the catfish has very tough skin, which should be removed before cooking. Tom, Joe, and Huck would have been very familiar with the catfish-skinning process. Allow plenty of time.

To skin a catfish:
First, eviscerate the fish. Then drive a nail through a board that is long enough to be held down firmly with a hand or knee while skinning the fish. Turn the board so the nail is sticking up and impale the head of the fish on the nail. Holding the board with one hand and working with the other, cut away enough of the skin from behind the head so you can grip it with a pair of pliers. With the pliers, start pulling the skin away from the flesh. It won't come off all in one piece.

After the skinning is completed, fry the bacon in a heavy skillet, preferably cast iron. Dredge the fish in corneal, drop it into the hot skillet, and fry until done. Serve with the bacon and corn pones.
Yield: 2 servings

DOUGHNUTS

Most people these days have never tasted a real made-from-scratch doughnut. Nearly every doughnut shop uses a mix, and who makes them at home? A real old-time doughnut, though, bears little resemblance to the flimsy imitations peddled in most bakeshops. Once you've tried homemade, your mouth will never again water at the sight of a tray full of the frosted styrofoam we've come to accept

3 ¼	cups sifted flour
2	teaspoon baking powder
½	teaspoon cinnamon
¼	teaspoon nutmeg
2	eggs
	vegetable shortening for frying
2/3	cups sugar
1	teaspoon vanilla

2/3   cups milk

¼   cup melted butter

a cup or so of mixed sugar and cinnamon to dust the doughnuts

Sift together the flour, baking powder and spices. Beat the eggs with the sugar in a separate bowl and add the vanilla to this mixture. Stir together the milk and melted butter. You should now have three different bowls of ingredients. Using the egg mixture as the base, add from the other two bowls alternately, beating after each addition. Cover the dough and chill it for at least an hour.

Roll out the dough until it is 1/2 inch thick, and cut with a doughnut cutter.

Melt enough solid shortening for several inches of fat in a deep frying pan. The temperature should be at about 375 degrees. Fry the doughnuts only a few at a time, turning once. Drain on paper towels.

Put the cinnamon-sugar in a medium paper bag and shake the doughnuts in it a few at a time to coat.

Yield: 18 doughnuts

BAT-EATING

Injun Joe, buried alive in the cave and starving, resorted to eating bats, as evidenced by the claws scattered near his body. Although I've never seen a recipe for them, fruit bats are eaten in some parts of the world and like many so-called delicacies, reportedly taste like chicken.

ALICE IN WONDERLAND AND THROUGH THE LOOKING GLASS

by
Lewis Carroll

In the Victorian period, when most children's books strove to instruct the young in morality, the books of Lewis Carroll entertained his readers by turning the seemingly rational adult world upside down with word play, conundrums and nonsense poetry, whose chief aim was to tickle. The limits of time and space are broken, memory is of the future instead of the past, and little girls are able to grow alternately large and small by sampling a bite of currant cake or a bottle of drink that tastes of "cherry-tart, custard, pineapple, roast turkey, toffee, and hot buttered toast."

Among his personal writings, Lewis Carroll has left us a commentary on his fantastical stories, *Alice in Wonderland* and *Through the Looking Glass.*

> Query: When we are dreaming, as so often happens, have a dim consciousness of the fact and try to wake, do we not say and do things which in waking life would be insane? May we not then sometimes feel insanity's an inability to distinguish which is the waking and which the sleeping life? We often dream without the least suspicion of unreality: "Sleep hath its own world," and it is often as lifelike as the other.

Lewis Carroll tests the reader's suspension of disbelief as we embark on a tour of the netherside of Victorian restraint to a world where chaos flourishes and absurdity reigns.

The fanciful creatures Alice encounters on her journey include a snap-dragon-fly whose "body is made of plum pudding, its wings of holly leaves, and its head is a raisin burning in brandy." It makes its nest in a Christmas box and lives on frumenty and mince pie. And crawling at her feet, Alice spies a bread-and-butter-fly whose wings are slices of bread and butter. Its head is a lump of sugar and it feeds mainly on tea with cream.

But Wonderland is made not only of the sugarplum dreams of children, it also contains nightmare images of an irrational, meaningless adult world where logic has no power and life no consistent form. Alice is taken prisoner, a baby suddenly turns into a pig and scampers off into the dark wood, live flamingos are used as croquet mallets, and riddles have no answers. The mock turtle—the main ingredient of mock turtle soup—sobs his tale of studying "reeling and writhing, uglification and derision."

Carroll was the first to use the chessboard as a metaphor for life. Alice is unable to see the entire game from her place on the board. She is a pawn, and like the other characters, never grasps the game. Alice is doomed never to understand her own experience. Looking down on this irrational, rude, and even violent world is the Cheshire Cat, having disappeared, all but his ironic grin.

Lewis Carroll, a fastidious Oxford mathematics don, originally told the story of Alice's adventures in Wonderland to the three Liddell sisters—Alice, Lorina, and Edith—at a riverbank picnic, a day Carroll remembered 25 years later as

> that "golden afternoon" that gave thee (Alice in Wonderland) birth, but I can call it up as clearly as if it were yesterday—the cloudless blue above, the watery mirror below, the boat drifting idly by on its way, the tinkle of the drops that fell from the oars, as they waved so sleepily to and fro, and (the one bright gleam of life in all the slumberous scenes) the three eager faces, hungry for news of fairy-land.

It was at the request of Alice, Carroll's favorite Liddell, that he wrote the story down and illustrated it, originally calling it *Alice's Adventures Under Ground*.

Carroll was a child-doting bachelor who had a particular fondness for little girls. Over the years he made friends with many children, with whom he kept up a prodigious correspondence. He was a master of mirror, or backward writing, and often sent his letters in that form so the recipient would have to hold the letter up to a looking glass in order to read it. This was probably the inspiration for the title to the sequel of *Alice in Wonderland, Through the Looking Glass*.

The meticulous Carroll, whose given name was Charles Lutwidge Dodgson, was a model of Victorian propriety and order, fussing endlessly about the state of his summer gloves, carefully organizing and filing the thousands of letters he received over his lifetime, and keeping an exact account of every meal served to every guest in his 47 years at Oxford so that no one would be served the same meal twice. Although Carroll himself was largely a disinterested eater, taking only a biscuit and a glass of wine at lunch, no matter the occasion, as the curator of the Senior Common Room at Christ Church he was said to have been easily agitated over the state of the cauliflower that regularly appeared on the menu there.

He traveled little outside England, making only one trip abroad, to Russia, which apparently made little impression on him, since he rarely referred to it in his extensive journals and letters. Most of his attention was given to fiddling with the newest gadgets of the day, including the camera. In addition to his careers as writer and mathematics teacher, Dodgson was also one of the foremost amateur photographers of his day.

Besides his children's fantasies, Dodgson was also the author of several books on mathematics. The man who devoted much of his life to analyzing Euclid's twelfth axiom and who drew a detailed diagram of how packages should be wrapped and knots tied, documents which hung in the mail room of his publishers for years, also reveled in the chaos of Wonderland, where queens swam in soup tureens, plum cake had a will of its own, and mutton pies were made of butterflies.

000

SNAP-DRAGON-FLY

The Snap-Dragon-Fly, which is said to eat frumenty and mince pies, could itself make a clever dessert for a Christmas party for either children or adults. Carroll left explicit directions for assembling one: A body of sliced plum pudding, wings of holly leaves, and a burning raisin for a head. Nested on a plate of Christmas paper, it is a festive finish to a holiday meal.

FRUMENTY

Frumenty, or fermenty as it is also known, is a porridge that was served on Christmas Eve in Medieval times, and is an ancestor of the treasured Christmas plum pudding. The transformation from porridge to pudding began when cooks started adding an egg yolk to the hot cereal. Over time they added more ingredients, such as dried fruits and spices, and began boiling the mixture in a pudding bag. Meanwhile, frumenty, the original dish, continued to be served, especially in the nursery.

1½	cups of whole wheat kernels (wheatberries)
2-2/3	cups water
½	teaspoon salt
	a handful of raisins

Soak the wheatberries in the water 8 to 10 hours or overnight. Bring the wheat and water mixture to a boil, add the salt and simmer until the kernels are soft. This takes about an hour. Add the raisins about 1/2 hour before you take it off the stove. Serve with any sweetening and milk or cream.
Yield: 4 to 6 servings

HOMEMADE MINCEMEAT

This recipe for homemade mincemeat makes enough for at least 18 pies, and keeps for a long time if stored in a cold place.

2	pounds cooked lean beef, chopped or ground
1	pound chopped beef fat
4	pounds chopped apples

3	pounds sugar
2	pounds currants
2	pounds raisins
1	whole nutmeg grated
½	teaspoon ground mace
	juice of 2 oranges and 2 lemons
½	pound candied citron

Combine all the ingredients and cook over low heat for two hours, stirring frequently. Pack into a stone crock, cover, and store in a cold place.
Yield: About 18 pies

MINCE PIE

Preheat oven to 450 degrees F.
Line a pan with your favorite pie crust dough. Fill with mincemeat. Cover with a top crust and bake for 30 minutes or until golden brown. Yield: 1 pie

Even though both plum pudding and its sister, plum cake, are studded with raisins and various other dried and candied fruits, neither contains plums. Originally, however, recipes for both called for prunes, the dried form of the plum. Later, as raisins and currants became easily available, cooks began using them instead, but the original name stuck.

This early recipe for plum cake produces a rather dry result, but you can add an egg or two to the batter if you want a moister cake.

PLUM CAKE

Preheat oven to 350 degrees F.

2	cups flour
1	cup sugar
1	cup dried currants

¼	cup candied lemon peel
½	cup soft butter
1	cup milk
1	teaspoon baking soda

Mix together the flour, sugar, currants, lemon peel and baking soda. Beat in the soft butter and milk. Turn the batter into a buttered baking tin and bake 1-1/2 hours or until the cake tests done.

Mutton, the meat of a grown sheep, is very fatty and requires aging. It is rarely available in the United States, but our lamb, somewhat older than that sold in Britain, is an adequate substitute. This savoury pie is a good leftover dish for roast lamb.

MUTTON PIE

Preheat oven to 450 degrees

3	cups any combination of leftover lamb or mutton, gravy, cooked vegetables, chopped onion, and parsley, meat or vegetable broth, or water to moisten if desired.
2	tablespoons flour mixed with 1/4 cup water

Pastry dough for a single crust pie

Slowly cook together the meat, vegetables and broth or gravy until the meat is very tender. Add the flour and water mixture if the gravy is too thin. Stir until blended and thickened. Fill a casserole or other baking dish with the meat mixture. Cover with the pie crust and cut slits in it to release the steam. Bake about 15 minutes or until browned.

ANNA KARENINA

by
Leo Tolstoy

Tolstoy's epic novel of illicit love, *Anna Karenina*, is the story not only of the unsanctified marriage of Anna and her lover, Vronsky, but also of Levin, the philosophical landowner whose character speaks for the author. Originally titled *Two Couples*, and later *Two Marriages*, the novel traces the relationship of the extraordinarily beautiful and sophisticated Anna and her handsome-but-shallow lover, Count Vronsky, and that of the serious, soul-searching Levin and his virtuous and wholesome young wife, Kitty, who have rejected the corrupting influences of society to live in the country (thus illustrating Tolstoy's own newly embraced views of living.)

Tolstoy underwent a prolonged spiritual search while writing *Anna Karenina*. Like his character Levin, Tolstoy was very much at ease with the peasants who worked on his ancestral estate, Yasnaya Polyana (Bright Meadow), preferring what he perceived as the free and natural life of the country to the trappings of so-called sophisticated urban society. As happens to Levin in the novel, Tolstoy's own quest ended with a profound religious commitment. Tolstoy came to believe that the essential message of the Gospels was to live as "natural" a life as possible. This included rejecting the artificiality of society and dedicating oneself not to self-gratification, but seeking God in the simplest of everyday activities. He believed that private ownership of property was a main source of evil in the world, and that all work and the fruits of labor should be shared. A dedicated debauchee in his youth, Tolstoy began to preach against carnal lust and thought elaborate food to be corrupting. He eventually became a vegetarian, gave up alcohol and tobacco, and in a most unhedonistic gesture, began to make his own shoes.

In the novel, Levin and Kitty, with their wholesome country life of physical labor and simple pursuits, represent that path which leads to virtue and salvation. The other characters, associated as they are with city life, the vapid world of the leisure class, and the spirit-deadening quality of the bureaucratic society, provide contrast to Tolstoy's view that in order to live a satisfying life, one must act according to one's own most natural instincts.

On one of his rare visits to Moscow, Levin agrees to dine with his friend Oblonsky in a fashionable restaurant. They start by helping themselves to fish and vodka at the sideboard, the traditional way a Russian meal begins, and Levin feels revulsion for the heavily made-up, perfumed Frenchwoman behind the counter, a grotesque perversion of Levin's (and Tolstoy's) ideal woman: pure, natural, in happy harmony at the center of the family circle. The author continues his condemnation of the artificiality of the aristocracy as the two men are presented with the bill of fare. Although Oblonsky insists on ordering the rich delicacies of the aristocratic palate—oysters, clear soup, turbot with sauce *Beaumarchais, poulard à la estragon, macedoine de fruits*—Levin says he would actually prefer cabbage soup and porridge.

Levin is ill at ease in all the fuss of the restaurant: the crystal, the mirrors, the bustle of waiters. He finds the environment contaminating, full as he is of thoughts of marriage and children and the purity of country living. It seems queer, he says, that country people eat their meals with dispatch so that they can get back to work, while here in the city the object seems to be to drag the meal out as long as possible. "Why of course," objects Oblonsky, "but that's just the aim of civilization—to make everything a source of enjoyment."

Levin is at his happiest among his peasant laborers, who do not trouble themselves with the elaborate refinements to which the upper classes are such slaves. When mowing time comes, Levin works alongside the other men, his hand on the scythe, moving rhythmically, without self-consciousness. He empties his mind of thought, allowing the rise and fall of his body to imitate the rise and fall of life: birth and death, planting and harvest. He takes his energy from the sun beating down on his back, and his refreshment from water dipped from a stream with leaves floating in it, and the perfume of the new-mown grass. He feels that some external force is moving him, and he gives himself completely to the moment until dinner is brought to the fields by bands of laughing children. Although a finer meal awaits Levin in his dining room, he joyfully shares an old peasant's "sop"—moistened bits of bread and sour rye beer.

When the urbane Oblonsky returns Levin's visit, Levin characteristically invites him to dine in simplicity in his country home. They start with bread, salted mushrooms and goose. They eat so much of the first course that Levin orders the nettle soup to be served without the little pies that the cook takes particular pride in, and although Stepan Oblonsky is used to much more refined meals, he pronounces everything splendid—the bread, the mushrooms, the chicken, the white Crimean wine, and the herb-brandy—as he lights a fat cigar, though his friend does not join him in this last pleasure. "How is it that you don't smoke?" Oblonsky says, "a cigar is a sort of thing, not exactly a pleasure, but the crown and outward sign of pleasure." Levin, though, finds such a habit superfluous at best. His quest is not for the pleasures life offers, but for the meaning in life, and he prefers not to waste his time in useless activity.

The novel contrasts those who spend their lives as pleasure seekers with those who instead seek meaning. The exquisitely beautiful Anna Karenina and her lover live in society, habitués of the grand balls and soirées, intended only for the pleasure of the guests. They fall into profane love and debase the sacrament of marriage, causing Anna to desert her legitimate son, whom she loves much, but perhaps not more, than her lover.

Kitty and Levin, on the other hand, find fulfillment in their union, which centers around their family, physical labor, and the smell and feel of the soil of their motherland. Only when one engages life on its simplest and most direct terms, Tolstoy tells us through Levin and Kitty, can one hope to find meaning.

The Russians actually invented the hors d'oeuvres course, which they call zakuski. It is often quite elaborate, and sometimes served in the drawing room with drinks before dinner. Levin and Oblonsky help themselves to zakuski from a common table of assorted preserved fish in the Moscow restaurant, while Levin serves only his local mushrooms, preserved with salt, at his country home. Levin and his guest feast so well on the delicious zakuski that Levin decides piroshki, the traditional savory pastry, will ruin their appetites for what is to come, and so dispenses with them for the second course: nettle soup.

CABBAGE PIROSHKI

Piroshki can be filled with almost any vegetable or meat combination and are a good way to use leftovers. Many types of dough can be used, and the piroshkis can be either baked or fried. The following sour cream pastry is very tender. These are filled with the ubiquitous cabbage.

Filling:

6	tablespoons oil
1	large onion, minced
1	pound cabbage finely shredded
4	teaspoons dried dill weed
1	tablespoon salt
	black pepper to taste
2	hard-boiled eggs, minced

Sauté the onions and the cabbage in the oil until the cabbage is tender, about 15 minutes. Mix the other ingredients and let the mixture cool.

Pastry:

3	cups flour
¾	teaspoon salt
2	tablespoon sugar

1   cup shortening or butter

¾   cup sour cream

Mix together the dry ingredients. Cut the butter in until the dough has the texture of cornmeal. Add the sour cream and mix thoroughly. Wrap in wax paper and chill for at least an hour. Preheat the oven to 375 degrees. Roll out the dough to 1/8 inch thickness. Using a 4-inch diameter cookie cutter, cut the dough into about 18 circles. Divide the filling among the circles, placing it on the side of each. Fold the other side over the filling to make a crescent shape, and crimp the edges tightly with a fork. Place on lightly greased cookie sheets and bake for about 30 minutes, or until golden brown.
Yield: 18 piroshkis

NETTLE SOUP

If you are lucky enough to find wild nettles—that pesky weed which is the bane of bare-legged hikers—gather them for soup, but be sure to wear gloves; they sting. Cooking, however, neutralizes them.

up to 1 quart young nettle tops

5 cups any soup stock

2 tablespoons uncooked rice

Wearing rubber gloves, remove the nettle tops from any woody stems. Add them to boiling stock, along with the rice. Simmer until the rice is done.
Yield: 4 servings

CABBAGE SOUP

Cabbage soup and porridge, which Levin holds in such high esteem, are often served together. Put a heaping spoonful of the porridge (made from buckwheat groats) in each bowl before adding the cabbage soup. Cabbage soup is cheap, easy to make, very tasty, and keeps you warm on cold, cold days.

2   quarts of any soup stock

1 ½   lbs. cabbage

1 ½   lbs. root vegetables such as carrots, potatoes, turnips, etc.

1   onion

1   celery stalk

1   sprig parsley

4   peppercorns

1   bayleaf

       salt to taste

       sour cream (optional)

Chop the cabbage, onion and parsley. Cut the root vegetables into julienne strips. Add all ingredients except the salt to the stock, bring to a boil, cover, and simmer for about an hour. Add salt 10 minutes before serving. Garnish with sour cream.
Yield: 6 to 8 servings

RUSSIAN PORRIDGE

Russian porridge is also called *kasha*, or buckwheat groats. It is extremely simple to cook, cheap, and nutritious.

1   cup buckwheat groats (*kasha*)

2   cups water

       dash of salt

Roast the kasha in a heavy saucepan without fat, stirring until it starts to pop. Add the water and salt, cover, and cook on very low heat until all of the water is absorbed, about 45 minutes. Yield: 2 servings

THE AWAKENING

by
Kate Chopin

New Orleans, that voluptuary of American cities—its air moist and heavy with the scents of jasmine and spicy Creole cooking, rich with the sounds of its intoxicating language, a mixture of Southern drawl and Creole French—is the setting for much of Kate Chopin's 1899 novel, *The Awakening*. This story of Edna Pontellier, a society belle who says she would give up anything but her *self* for her children, was banned and its author shunned by society in Chopin's native St. Louis.

Edna, the scandalous heroine of *The Awakening*, leaves behind her husband and children to take a small house of her own where she intends to develop her skills as both a painter and a lover. Edna's appetites for art and love are matched by her appetite for food.

While the style of the day was for a woman to be a delicate eater, Edna snacks on cheese and crackers and a bottle of beer after an unsatisfying dinner party, tears off chunks of crusty bread with her teeth, and takes hard liquor as she pleases. In this early feminist novel, eating is a metaphor for Edna's appetite for living. Married at an early age to a bourgeois businessman and relegated to the tasks of keeping a fashionable home on New Orleans' Esplanade Street, Edna longs for an independent existence. Appropriately, we often see her dining alone, perhaps in a secluded restaurant, perhaps at home. She relishes a supper of chops and strong coffee in a country cook house and nibbles *marrons glacés* in a comfortable peignoir at home. Edna is never the cook, but the sensuous table setting at a lavish dinner party to celebrate her move from her husband's home is her creation.

On the last night in her husband's house, Edna invites a select group of friends for the most glamourous meal of the story: the "*coup de etat* dinner," as her lover calls it. She serves a sparkling garnet-colored cocktail, but the aperitif course is the only one described in this most sensuous of meals; the author concentrates instead on the total effect of the table. The golden glow of Edna's satin gown compliments the arrangements of red and yellow roses, as candles shimmer through goblets of champagne. On the satin and lace tablecloth, the silver and French china glitter like the jewels on the women's breasts. The tinkle of laughter plays against the sound of the fountains and strains of a mandolin. Against this golden backdrop, the women, in a most un-victorian ritual, decorate a handsome young guest with a garland of roses made from the centerpiece and drape his dark suit with a silken scarf. Sipping champagne from their glasses, they see the boy as "a graven image of desire."

Edna's emancipation from the bindings of conventional society begins on Grand Isle, a summer resort of the Louisiana Gulf, populated mainly by women with children whose husbands commute on the weekends. The days are filled with knitting and the devouring of treasure boxes of bonbons, delicious syrups, and patés; the evenings are punctuated with moonlight swims, homemade ice cream served with slices of gold and silver cake, and the soughing of palm-leaf fans. At the end of one of these "mystic" evenings on the island, Edna finally learns to swim. She is heady with this new power, and for the first time feels in total control of "the working of her body and soul." Indeed, she feels reckless, desiring to "swim far out, where no woman had swum before." So overwhelmed is she by the exuberance that swimming gives her and the awakening of her desire for illicit love that she is unwilling to share her husband's bed, and spends the night in a hammock on the porch.

The next afternoon, faint from her sleepless night, Edna retires to a small country inn to recover. There she luxuriates in the feel of fresh country linens and the newly-discovered strength of her own body. She bathes, then slips into the laurel-scented bed. She runs her fingers through her long hair and examines her firmly textured arms before falling into a heavy and satisfying sleep.

Meanwhile, her male companion has foraged the island, and when she awakes he serves her a hearty Sunday supper of sizzling fowl, boiled mullets, and wine. He is gratified to see the gusto with which she eats under the orange-laden trees, draining her wine glass and brushing together the last crumbs of the crusty loaf.

000

"BOILED" MULLETS

Edna Pontellier often enjoys the delicately flavored fish of the Louisiana Gulf coast. In fact, her last act before her final determined swim in the all-embracing waves is to order fish for dinner. The following recipe for boiled mullets is much more flavorful than the name implies, for "boiled" is an old term for poached. One mullet per person makes a generous serving.

1	mullet per person
½	cup white wine
½	cup vinegar
1	rib celery
½	onion, stuck with 2 cloves
1	thinly sliced carrot
1	teaspoon thyme
8	peppercorns
1	bay leaf
1	sprig of parsley
6	cups of hot water

Combine the ingredients in a fish poacher and simmer 15 minutes. Cook only as many fish at a time as your liquid will adequately cover well. Cook each about 10 minutes, or until opaque. Liquid can be used several times.

MARRONS GLACES (GLACED CHESTNUTS)

4	cups chestnuts
4	cups water
4	cups sugar
1	tablespoon cream of tartar

Shell and skin the chestnuts, and soak in water to cover overnight. The next day, drop into boiling water and boil until tender. Drain and let sit while making syrup.

Boil together the sugar, water and the cream of tartar. Boil and stir until syrup just begins to change color. Remove the syrup from the heat and dip the chestnuts one by one, letting them dry on waxed paper. (The air may be too moist for them to dry this way; if so, they can be dried in a warm oven set below 100 degrees.)

Gold and silver cakes are named for the white and yolk of the dozen eggs each contains. When cooks of Kate Chopin's day made angel food cake, a "gold cake" soon followed. In memory of Edna's first swim, serve both with vanilla ice cream.

SILVER (ANGEL FOOD) CAKE

1	cup sifted cake flour
1½	cups sugar
12	egg whites
1½	teaspoons vanilla

Preheat oven to 375 degrees F.

Sift flour with half the sugar twice. Beat egg whites with vanilla until glossy, soft peaks form. Add remaining sugar gradually, beating until stiff peaks form. Sift flour over the whites in fourths, folding in each time. Bake in an ungreased tube pan at 375 degrees for 35 minutes. Invert pan until cool.

GOLD CAKE

12	egg yolks
2	cups powdered sugar
1	cup orange juice

1	teaspoon vanilla
2	cups sifted cake flour
2	teaspoons baking powder

Preheat oven to 325 degrees F.

Beat yolks with an electric mixer until lemon colored. Sift sugar three times and beat in gradually. Stir in orange juice and vanilla. Sift together flour and baking powder 4 times and fold into egg mixture. Bake in an ungreased tube pan for 50 to 60 minutes, or until the cake springs back when pressed. Invert to cool in pan.

CANNERY ROW

by
John Steinbeck

The gray dawn matches the iridescent gloom of the cannery buildings, reeking of yesterday's catch. An occasional ray of sun filters through to reflect off the metal rooftops, like the silver glint of the darting sardine. Mangy cats and dogs range the streets, looking for fish heads and other detritus of Monterey's Cannery Row. Beer caps sparkle in the sunlight, gentle breezes ruffle the trash in vacant lots as Mack and the boys settle into the Palace Flophouse for a long day's rest after a night of "punch," a mixture of the dregs of the customers' drinks at Eddie's sometime job as a bartender. As the day wears on, the air fills with the smell of frying pork chops for an early dinner down at Dora's, where the wide-hipped girls ready themselves for a night of sport.

This is life during the great depression as depicted in *Cannery Row*, John Steinbeck's affectionate memoir cherished by the free-spirited young in search of simpler, more partying times. In this symbiotic world, everything lives on the leavings of something else.

Mack and the boys and their canine and feline brothers are on the bottom half of the food chain that provides a place and function for all Cannery Row inhabitants. Everybody's looking for a score, and everybody at one time or another passes through Lee Chong's grocery, where a person can buy everything except the commodity sold across the lot at Dora's. The traffic is heavy in Lee Chong's, and one of his most frequent customers is the infamous "Doc," the quasi-biologist who owns and operates Western Biological Laboratory. Doc is a taker of specimens, giver of parties, connoisseur of the odd—and even the grotesque, in both food and women.

The character of Doc is based on the real-life character of Ed Ricketts, whom Steinbeck eulogizes at length in the prologue to *The Log of the Sea of Cortez*. It is almost impossible to separate Doc, the character, from Ed Ricketts, the man. Both are slight, bearded, and goat-like biologists with penchants for music, philosophy, and food. As Steinbeck says in his prologue, "Ed loved food, and many of the words he used were eating words." Women, as well as beer and blue cheese, were "delicious." And he was just as curious about marine life as he was about a beautiful woman. For instance, Steinbeck reports, "Ed had always wondered why other marine life never ate the beautiful and tasty looking nudibranch, so he once tasted one—fresh and lively from the tidepool—and instantly found out why. His immediate involuntary wince was a mild reaction compared to the occasion on which he couldn't close his mouth for 24 hours after tasting a species of free-swimming anemone and getting stung by its nettle cells."

Although Doc seems to exist mainly on beer, he actually supplements it with prodigious amounts of fried steak, canned sardines, pineapple pie, and one beer milkshake, served up by a blond beauty with just the hint of a goiter.

It was on a collecting trip to La Jolla to fill an order for small octopi that Doc invented the beer milkshake. He was up early to pack, comb and trim his beard, and wash three days' dishes. He loaded the car, shut the doors to the lab, and was on his way by 9 o'clock. Before he even got out of Monterey, he felt hungry and made his first stop of the day, Herman's, for a hamburger and a beer. Meditating over his meal, he became obsessed with the idea of a beer milkshake. "Doc didn't stop at Salinas for a hamburger. But he stopped in Gonzales, in King City, and Paso Robles. He had hamburger and beer at Santa Maria. In Santa Barbara he had soup, lettuce and string bean salad, pot roast and mashed potatoes, pineapple pie and blue cheese and coffee." So in Ventura he stopped only for beer. He walked straight up to the counter, looked the goitered blonde in the eye, and ordered a beer milkshake.

But the trip was not over yet, and the shake didn't quell his appetite. A couple of hours out of Ventura he had a cheese sandwich, followed by "a good dinner" in Los Angeles: fried chicken, julienne potatoes, hot biscuits and honey, and more pineapple pie and blue cheese. "...here he filled his thermos bottle with hot coffee, had them make up six ham sandwiches and bought two quarts of beer for breakfast." After pulling into La Jolla at 2 a.m. he had a sandwich, some more beer, and went to work.

As befits a man of his prodigious appetite, Ed Ricketts, the real-life Doc, died on the way to the market to get a good steak. His beat-up sedan stalled on the railroad tracks just at twilight, when it was most difficult for the engineer to see it in enough time to stop.

000

BEER MILKSHAKE

Although Doc's recipe for the beer milkshake is half milk, half beer, the addition of a scoop of vanilla ice-cream makes it taste something like a gin fizz.

¼   cup milk

1   scoop vanilla ice cream

½   bottle of a good light-colored beer (not the reduced calorie kind)

Put all ingredients in a blender and process until thoroughly mixed.
Yield: 2 servings

PINEAPPLE PIE

Begin with your favorite recipe for a single crust pie.

Filling:

2   cups canned crushed pineapple

2   heaping tablespoons cornstarch

2   tablespoons sugar

1   tablespoon butter

Place the pineapple in the top of a double boiler over simmering water. Blend the cornstarch and sugar and add to the pineapple. Cook and stir until thickened, about 20 minutes. Stir in butter. Add the filling to the crust when both have cooled completely.

MERINGUE

2   egg whites

¼   teaspoon vanilla

¼   cup sugar

Beat egg whites until soft peaks form and then beat in sugar and vanilla. Spread meringue over the filling, making sure the meringue covers it completely and touches the crust so that it does not shrink in baking. Bake the pie at 425 degrees for about five minutes, or until the meringue is nicely browned.

DAVID COPPERFIELD

by

Charles Dickens

Is there a literate person in all the western world who hears such titles as *A Christmas Carol, Oliver Twist,* or *David Copperfield* without thinking of roast goose, merry holly-decked puddings, and warming drinks at the fireside? The works of Charles Dickens abound with festive spirits, hearty fare, and pleasant company. His characters roam the vibrant streets of London, fortifying themselves with meat pies, cold puddings, and warm gingerbread. No sooner is a long-lost acquaintance restored but a table is laid and the poker set in the grate to mull whatever is handy.

In *David Copperfield,* much of the gustatory pleasures revolve around the comings and goings of the indigent Micawber family—a meal to drown one's sorrows, a little refreshment to mark a new venture, a celebration of the various recoveries in-between. Mrs. Micawber suffers the humiliation and degradation of her husband's irresponsible ways, but no sooner has she lain prostrate with grief than she is up eating chops and drinking warmed ale, paid for with another two teaspoons from her wedding set. While awaiting a remittance from London with which to pay their Canterbury hotel bill, the destitute Micawbers pass the time feasting on hot kidney pudding and plates of shrimp for breakfast. During a particularly difficult time for the Micawber household, as the furniture is hauled off piece by piece, Mrs. Micawber and young David Copperfield discuss the dim future over "a little jug of egg hot," a concoction of warmed beer, eggs, sugar, and nutmeg, especially comforting on a dark and chilly afternoon before a fire.

David is still a child in this scene, but already, like most of Dickens' boys, he is alone in the world and has been forced into adulthood much too soon. While he works at the bottlinghouse of Murdstone and Grinby, David nourishes himself on pennyloaves, cold puddings, and an occasional savaloy (a spicy, dry sausage.) Already accustomed to the currant and cowslip wine given to him by his nurse, Peggoty, David confidently enters a pub and orders a glass of "Genuine Stunning...with a good head to it" on the occasion of his birthday.

David's childhood drinking habits do not seem in the least unusual in a book awash with characters considerably the worse for their tippling. Mr. Wickfield, lost in his cups since his wife's death, is gradually pulled into the maw of the obsequious Uriah Heep. A former tenant at David's London bachelor digs died of drink, and Mrs. Crupp, the landlady, is also a victim of the pleasures of the punchbowl. But the red-nosed and verbose Mr. Micawber is probably the most memorable of these drinkers, particularly for his rum punch, a concoction capable of drowning sorrows, heralding some new venture, and celebrating anything that seems the least bit worthy of conviviality—often all three in the same evening.

Dickens' descriptions of Micawber border on the celestial when his feckless face shines out at the company from a cloud of steam "amid the fragrance of lemon peel and sugar, the odor of burning rum." He stirs, he mixes, and he tastes "as if he were making, instead of punch, a fortune for his family." With never a farthing to his name, Micawber is seldom more sure that "Something is bound to turn up" than he is at these moments.

Micawber does the bacchanalian honors at one of several dinner parties David presides over in the establishment of his valitudinous landlady, Mrs. Crupp. She takes a little brandy on occasion "for medicinal purposes," and does seem to have trouble completing her custodial duties. The menu at David's rather elaborate dinner to entertain his old acquaintance, Steerforth, is derived largely from what Mrs. Crupp cannot do. Her fireplace is "fitted out" only to do chops and mashed potatoes, her range not capable of poaching a fish. Never mind, however that "Oysters is in, why not them?" Her further recommendations include "A pair of hot roast fowls—from the pastry cook's, a tart, and...a shape of jelly (also) from the pastry cook's." Thus would Mrs. Crupp's mind be free to concentrate on the potatoes "and to serve up the cheese and celery as she would wish to see it done." All this to greet an old friend, along with an extravagant order from the wine merchant's, the last doubtless the inspiration for Dickens' chapter title, "My First Dissipation."

For his second dinner party, a *fete* to celebrate his reunion with the (by now) infamous Micawbers, a wiser and more sober David makes less extensive preparations: "(a) pair of soles, a small leg of mutton, and a pigeon pie." Bribed with David's promise to dine out for a fortnight afterwards, the ever-ailing Mrs. Crupp agrees to do the culinary honors.

After frying the two fish, however, the landlady loses her grip on the preparations, for the leg of mutton is pale without and red within, "besides having a foreign substance of a gritty nature sprinkled over it, as if it had had a fall into the ashes." In addition to mislaying the mutton, Mrs. Crupp has somehow left the gravy decorating the boardinghouse staircase, where it will remain for weeks to come, and the pigeon pie is sadly lacking in pigeon beneath its lumpy crust. In short, as Mr. Micawber would say, "...the god of day has gone down upon the dreary scene and left us forever floored."

But the penurious Micawber, accustomed to rallying his spirits and making do in his pecuniary disasters, saves the evening by suggesting the entire party cooperate in the making of a "Devil," a spiced and grilled meat popular in Victorian times. David's friend Traddles sets about slicing the heretofore mistreated mutton. Micawber "covered them with pepper, mustard, salt and cayenne; I put them on the gridiron, turned them with a fork, and took them off, under Mr. Micawber's directions, and Mrs. Micawber heated "...some mushroom ketchup in the little saucepan." The "novelty" and "bustle" of this cookery, the tucking into their supper in shirtsleeves, the getting up to turn the sputtering and blazing slices, the sitting back down to another bite only to get up again to retrieve the finished slices of meat adds to the conviviality. Traddles laughs heartily throughout, we are told, and the Micawbers "couldn't have enjoyed it more if they had sold a bed to pay for it."

000

Bustle is not a word most of us would care to have applied to our dinner parties, so I do not recommend you enlist the aid of your guests to quite the degree David does. Instead, give them a warming cup of rum punch or egg nog and put them beside a cheery fire while you prepare the following simple recipes from Mr. Micawber's collection.

MR. MICAWBER'S RUM PUNCH

1	teaspoon sugar
	rum to taste
	boiling water
1	slice of lemon

Place the sugar in a ceramic mug. Fill 2/3 full with boiling water. Add rum to taste and garnish with lemon.
Yield: 1 serving

EGG HOT

2	bottles of quality ale, each 12 ounces
2	teaspoons sugar
1	pinch of mace
1	pat of butter
1	beaten egg

In a saucepan, mix the ale, sugar, mace and butter. Heat until the butter is melted. Whisk the egg into the mixture until frothy and serve at once.
Yield: 2 servings

DEVILED LAMB

Since mutton is rarely available in the United States, spread any cut of lamb chops with a mixture of black pepper, prepared mustard (preferably Dijon), salt, and cayenne. Broil or grill until sputtering. Serve with warm mushroom ketchup.

MUSHROOM KETCHUP

1   quart fresh mushrooms

        salt

½   teaspoon powdered cloves

12   grinds of pepper

2   teaspoons vinegar

        olive oil

Layer fresh mushrooms in a crock, salting each layer liberally. Let stand in a cool place for 4 days. Drain and mash until fine. Add cloves, pepper and vinegar. Place the crock in a pan of water and boil about 2 hours. Cool and puree the mixture in a blender until smooth. Store in refrigerator, covered with a layer of olive oil. It should keep for a couple of weeks.

"THE DEAD"

by
James Joyce

James Joyce's *The Dead* opens at the annual holiday dance, given by Gabriel Conroy's elderly maiden aunts who, in spite of their modest living as music teachers, never stint themselves or their guests. They serve "the best of everything: diamond-bone sirloins, three-schilling tea and the best bottled stout." The yearly party includes everyone they know: family, friends, pupils, members of the choir. Nearly the entire flat is given over to the festivities. Refreshment tables are set up and rooms are cleared to make space for dancing. Those who are so inclined perform traditional Irish songs or piano pieces, and somewhere before midnight everyone sits down to a magnificent holiday feast.

There is stuffed goose, ham "peppered" over with crumbs, and spiced beef at the ends of the table. Between them are "two little minsters of jelly, red and yellow, blocks of blancmange and red jam, a large green leaf-shaped dish with a stalk-shaped handle, on which lay bunches of purple raisins and peeled almonds," Smyrna figs, custard topped with grated nutmeg, chocolates in gold and silver papers, and a glass vase of tall celery stalks. In the center "as sentries to a fruit stand which upheld a pyramid of oranges and American apples, two squat old-fashioned decanters of cut glass, one containing port and the other dark sherry." And still more is loaded onto the piano: A pudding and "three squads of bottles of stout and ale and minerals, drawn according to the colors of their uniforms, the first two black, with brown and red labels, the third and smallest squad white, with transverse green sashes."

Lily, the housemaid, circulates around the table with "Hot floury potatoes wrapped in a white napkin" while the goose is carved. The guests chatter of music and bygone tenors as the food is passed around and they urge each other on in their eating and their conversation. Gradually, the sweets are passed, the last glasses filled, and the chairs resettled. The conversation dwindles, and finally ceases. Gabriel Conroy, the favorite of the old aunts, begins his traditional after-dinner speech. His subject is Irish hospitality, unique in the world and, some would say, more a failing than a virtue. The good sisters Morkan, their warm hearted hostesses, keep this generosity alive, offering to their guests (or, teases Gabriel, "had I better say victims?") the tradition of hospitality handed down by their forebears.

The theme of hospitality seems to have been strongly on Joyce's mind at the writing of *The Dead*. In a letter from Italy to his brother shortly before beginning work on the story, he mentions that in all his travels on the Continent he has never encountered a people as hospitable as the Irish. Joyce bolsters the effect of Gabriel's speech by immediately preceding it with a discussion among the guests of the Mount Melleray monks, who never ask payment for the room and board they extend to any who wish to visit their monastery. Gabriel goes on to speak of the importance of camaraderie and the worth of good fellowship.

Gabriel worried over this speech earlier in the evening, wondering if much of what he has planned to say will be above the heads of his audience. Gabriel is a teacher at the university, a reviewer of books, well-traveled, and he often has difficulty, as he puts it, "striking the right tone with people." Upon arriving at the party, he receives a rebuff from Lily, the maid, when he attempts small talk with her and condescendingly offers a Christmas tip; his uneasiness is also apparent in his halting seduction of his wife, Gretta. He adopts an offhand tone to tell her that he lent the inebriate, Freddie Malins, money, in the hope of ingratiating himself with her. Despite these small monetary offers, the self-conscious Gabriel is not by nature a generous man. Even as Gretta compliments him on his generosity, he restrains himself from brutally castigating the whole Malins clan. Gabriel's discomfort in the bourgeoise company of his aunts' party and his attempts to seem generous, even to his wife, raise a question in the reader's mind as to what exactly he means when he teasingly refers to the generosity of his countrymen and women as a "failing." Perhaps he feels that because of the strong traditions and expectations of Irish society, he must behave in a socially-prescribed generous and open-hearted manner, even when it does not represent his own feelings.

It is near dawn before the party breaks up. Slushy snow creaks underfoot, the horse-drawn cab moves wearily through the darkness toward the hotel, and Gabriel's body pulses with longing for his still-beautiful wife. In the dim light of their room, Gabriel hesitates, hoping for a sign of her desire.

But his wife is not thinking of him. Instead, she tells him the story of a boy who once loved her, who died for her, and of the song tonight that reminded her of their friendship long ago. Humiliated by "this figure from the dead," he feels a fool, "a pennyboy for his aunts, a nervous well-meaning sentimentalist, orating to vulgarians and idealizing his own clownish lusts."

Later, after she has fallen asleep, Gabriel considers the story, and "generous" tears fill his eyes as he seems to mourn the death of the youthful lover. He watches the snow falling outside, imagining it drifting over the treeless hills, the "dark central plain," dusting the boy's grave, falling upon all of Ireland, on the living as well as the dead.

000

SPICED BEEF

Spiced beef is an Irish version of sauerbraten. It should be marinated for at least 12 hours, but up to several days is better, if you have the time. It is good served hot or cold.

4 to 5	lb. chuck roast
1	teaspoon each cinnamon, allspice and cloves
1 ½	teaspoons salt
1	teaspoon black pepper
2	sliced onions
1/2	bay leaf
	vinegar to cover
2	cups water

Cover the roast with all the above ingredients except the water. Marinate, covered, in the refrigerator for at least 12 hours.

Preheat the oven to 275 degrees F. Drain the meat and put it in a roasting pan. Heat half of the marinade and the water to boiling. Pour over the meat, cover, and roast for about 3 hours. Yield: 16-20 servings

HAM PEPPERED WITH CRUMBS

A country ham, such as would have been likely in Joyce's Dublin, needs boiling before it is glazed, and baked in order to reduce the amount of fat and salt and to be sure it is thoroughly cooked. If you are lucky enough to have a country ham, scrub it carefully with soap and water, taking care to rinse thoroughly, then soak it in water for 14 to 48 hours. Change the water, bring it to a boil, skim, and then simmer for 20 minutes per pound. It is now ready to be glazed and baked.

Hams bought in U.S. supermarkets do not ordinarily need these preliminary preparations. They may be glazed and baked directly from the package for 15 minutes per pound at 325 degrees, or as the manufacturer directs. These hams are often much smaller than country hams and sometimes are sold split into half or quarter pieces.

The following recipe makes enough glaze for a 4 to 5 pound piece, but can be easily increased for a larger ham.

1	4 to 5 lb. ham
2	teaspoons prepared mustard
1/3	cup bread crumbs
¾	cup brown sugar

One hour before the ham is due to come out of the oven, remove it and cut off the rind, leaving as much or as little fat as desired. Mix together crumbs, mustard, and brown sugar. Rub this mixture over the ham and return it to the oven until done.
Yield: 16-20 servings

BLANCMANGE

Blancmange is also known as "cornstarch pudding" in the United States and can be flavored with vanilla or rum, as well as almond, but the original is a delicate dessert made with ground blanched almonds. In this age of food processors and blenders, it is much easier to make than it once was. Chill it in your prettiest serving dish, and spoon out to serve.

½	pound blanched almonds
¾	cup water
¾	cup milk
1	tablespoon gelatin
¼	cup water
1	cup heavy cream
½	cup sugar
1	tablespoon kirsch

Grind the almonds to a course meal in a food processor. Combine the milk and the 3/4 cup of water in a bowl; add the almond meal, and let soak for up to an hour. Soak the gelatin in the 1/4 cup of water for 5 minutes. Mix the cream and sugar, and heat until scalded. Dissolve the gelatin mixture in the cream and sugar. Add the almond milk and stir. Add the kirsch and stir again. Chill until set and serve with red jam.

Yield: 6 servings

IRISH PLUM PUDDING

4	slices of fresh white bread cubes
1	cups milk
2	eggs
1	cup brown sugar
¼	cup any Guiness, stout or porter
6	ounces beef suet, finely minced
1	teaspoon vanilla
1	cup sifted flour
1	teaspoon baking soda
¼	teaspoon salt
2	teaspoons ground cinnamon
2	teaspoons ground cloves
1	teaspoon mace
2	cups raisins
1	cup pitted dates
½	cup citron
½	cup walnuts

Thoroughly soak the bread cubes in the milk, then beat until well-combined. You should have a smooth batter. Stir in the eggs, sugar, Guinness, suet, and vanilla. Sift together the flour, soda, and spices. Stir in the fruits and nuts first, then add the bread and milk mixture.

Pour into a well-buttered pudding mold. Secure the lid or cover tightly with foil, tying with string. Place the mold on a rack in a deep pot, containing an inch or so of boiling water. Cover the larger pot, and steam pudding for 3 to 4 hours, being sure to add more water if necessary. You might keep a kettle of boiling water available to add to your pot if necessary. The water should continue to simmer throughout the process. Remove the pudding mold from the kettle, and let it stand for 10 minutes before unmolding.

Yield: at least 6 servings

THE DEATH OF THE HEART

by
Elizabeth Bowen

Elizabeth Bowen's *The Death of the Heart* is one of the many British novels about an orphaned youngster who is valiantly trying to get a foothold in the world. Sixteen-year-old Portia has spent a vagabond existence with her parents, shifting from seedy hotel to borrowed flat, drifting about the Continent in permanent exile from the rest of the family. She belongs nowhere, knows no one. Her half-brother Thomas and his wife Anna have agreed to take charge of her welfare on a trial basis, and the novel depicts their emotional gropings in their first attempts to make a life together after the death of Portia's mother and father.

Unlike Portia's unstable but open-hearted parents, Thomas and Anna have difficulty expressing emotions and perhaps do not have them. Anna wanted children early in their marriage, but after two miscarriages she became fearful of another failure. This fear of failure is reflected in other aspects of her life as well. She had at one time hoped to become an interior decorator, but stopped after her first few clients lest she prove herself ultimately unsuccessful. She never deeply involves herself with people because she is afraid of the emotional risks involved.

Thomas also appears to be emotionally repressed, has no interest outside his business, and few friends. Certainly much of his reticence stems from his parents' relationship.

While Thomas was a young man away at Oxford, his father awakened his wife at 2 o'clock one morning and told her that he had completely lost his head over a very young woman and that she was now pregnant. In perhaps one of the most chilling reactions in literature, his wife of over 20 years cheerfully stopped her husband's crying, went downstairs, and in a typically British gesture made tea. She then announced that he would, of course, have to marry the young woman, turned him out of his beloved home, and began divorce proceedings. After Portia was born, the first Mrs. Quayne insisted that her son visit his father and new family regularly. She behaved "splendidly"—never faltered, never lost her composure, never exhibited a shred of emotion.

The story opens at Windsor Terrace, Thomas and Anna's house, where Portia—lonely and only tolerated—is seen as a symbol of Thomas's father's passion, and a source of embarrassment. The first paragraph describes a cold and bleak landscape: "that morning's ice…cracked and floating in segments." This is winter in London; cold and ice set the tone for the relationships among the characters. But the book moves with consistent fluidity from discord to resolution, from a houseful of characters alienated from one another to a sense that family unity is possible at Windsor Terrace.

The various settings in Bowen's novel represent aspects of the psyche. Windsor Terrace is a place of locked doors where people communicate chiefly by telephone, never deigning to confront one another. Matchett, the housekeeper and Portia's confidante, keeps the rooms antiseptically clean. It is the world of the repressed psyche, a symbol of life turned in on itself.

When Thomas and Anna holiday on Capri, Portia is sent to stay with a Mrs. Heccomb and family. The Heccomb's live on the Kentish coast in a sprawling claptrap of a house with the unlikely name of Waikiki. As exuberant as Windsor Terrace is restrained, Waikiki is a house beaten by rain and the storms that rage at sea. One hears life in the noisy plumbing and smells it in roasting meat. Public and private selves do not stand aloof from one another here. Whereas Anna, the former interior decorator, sends a visitor's pink carnations to the servant's quarters because they are the wrong color, Waikiki's broken doorbell greets Portia, immediately admitting to imperfection. While life is a deep, quiet pool at Portia's London residence, sensibilities splash on the surface at Waikiki.

Life is measured out in cups of tea in this novel. A warm cup comforts the lonely, distracts the bored, gives courage to the fearful, marks occasions, and punctuates the day. The rhythm of the domestic activity comes to a dramatic pause to accommodate the ritual: "...she had entered one of those pauses in the life of a house that before tea time seem to go on and on." It is at tea that Bowen's characters seem to reveal themselves the most. A cup of tea fortifies the first Mrs. Quayne when she learns of her husband's indiscretion and helps her to begin to cope with the coming changes in her life. Lonely and feeling like an intruder in her half-brother's home, Portia often has tea belowstairs with the matronly and attentive Matchett; it is a cozy affair of toast-making and confidences.

At tea with Anna and Thomas, everyone is nervous, and they have nothing to say to one another. Anna, Portia observes, has people in to tea who don't know if they should talk to Portia, who make no impression on Anna, and on whom Anna makes no impression.

Typically, tea at Waikiki is a disorganized affair—gramophone blaring, cakes slipped from bags onto plates at the last minute. Here, eating takes precedence over conversation. The Heccombs focus on activity, rather than style. They enjoy the act of eating their tea in all their unrepressed glory.

In her loneliness, Portia develops a crush on Eddie—protégé to Anna and a social climber who hasn't been out of debt in years. Eddie concerns himself only with superficial matters and does not give Portia the love and human warmth she so craves. Symbolically, Eddie and Portia meet for tea at Madam Tussaud's Waxworks, where Portia is disappointed to find that all the waitresses are real. The wax figures, she observes, must all be in another part of the building. In their conversation over tea and crumpets, Eddie explains that everyone he knows except Portia makes him feel he has got to "sing for his supper" and that he gets along by being what others want him to be. He sells himself on the social marketplace for invitations, a place to stay, and a small job here and there in order to support himself in the society to which he aspires.

000

The foods served at tea time—light sandwiches, various cakes, scones, and Portia's favorite, crumpets—are the comfort foods of England. Tea first became fashionable as a form of entertainment in the seventeenth century when the custom was brought from the Netherlands, where every fine home had its own tearoom. England's combination of a heavy breakfast, a light lunch, and dinner at eight left a vacant spot in the late afternoon, and in the stomachs of the aristocracy, thus the five o'clock consumption of refreshments became an opportunity for socializing.

PERFECT TEA

To make a perfect pot of tea, bring the water to a rolling boil, then rinse the teapot with some of the boiling water to warm it. Put in the pot one teaspoon of loose tea (never tea bags) for every six ounces of water. Pour in the boiling water, and let steep for about five minutes.

To Americans, crumpets are the quintessential ingredient of an English tea. Made from a batter somewhat thicker than that used for pancakes but thinner than for English muffins, they may, in fact, be the origin of these two distinctly American favorites. (English muffins, like French toast, appear to be a U.S. invention.)

Because the batter is thinnish, you may want to use rings so the crumpets will have an even, round shape. Make your own rings by removing both ends from cans of the size tuna is usually sold in and scrub the cans thoroughly.

CRUMPETS

1 ¾	cup scalded milk
1	cup hot water
2	teaspoons sugar
1	teaspoon salt
1	cake yeast
4	cups sifted flour
3	teaspoons soft butter

Have all liquid ingredients and butter at about 75 degrees F. Combine milk, water, sugar, and salt in a mixing bowl. Then add the yeast, and let it dissolve in the mixture for about ten minutes. Beat two cups of the flour gradually into the milk mixture. Cover the bowl with a damp cloth and set to allow the dough to rise in a warm place for about 1-1/2 hours. Beat in the soft butter. Mix in the rest of the flour, cover again, and put to rise until double in bulk. After the dough has risen for the second time, fill the rings about half full, and let them stand another hour or so for a final rising. Heat a griddle on the stove top at medium high heat, butter the griddle, place the crumpets on it, and bake until lightly browned on both sides. After cooling, toast like you would an English muffin and serve with butter, jam or marmalade.
Yield: 10 large crumpets

Tea in the English countryside is often heavier than what is served in town to accommodate the needs of men who have been laboring all day and who need something more substantial than cucumber sandwiches. Even in families without laborers, the tradition continues. The egg pie, served at Waikiki, is a plain quiche which can be served hot, cold, or at room temperature. You can add whatever leftovers are in the refrigerator—cheese, meats, vegetables—to give variety.

EGG PIE

1 ¼   cups milk

3   eggs

        a pinch of ground pepper

1   tablespoon butter

An 8 inch partially baked pastry shell

Preheat oven to 375 degrees

If desired, spread leftovers in shell. Beat together the milk, eggs, and pepper. Pour into the pastry shell. Cut the butter into very small pieces and distribute over the top. Bake for about 30 minutes. Cool 10 minutes before serving.

Eddie's favorite foods, he tells Portia, are jellied consommé and cheese straws. Cheese straws are easy to make, absolutely delicious, and are excellent at either tea or cocktails.

CHEESE STRAWS

½   pound cheddar cheese

3   tablespoons soft butter

2   tablespoons cold water

¾   cup flour

        dash of Tabasco sauce

Preheat oven to 475 degrees F.

Grate the cheese and combine with the other ingredients to make a dough similar in consistency to pie crust. A food processor works very well for this. Fill a cookie press and use the ribbon disk to make ribbons, then cut them into thin "straws." If you don't have a cookie press, you can use your hands to form straws, although they do turn out less "straw-like" with this method. Bake for 10 minutes.
Yield: about 3 dozen cheese straws.

*Jellied Consommé is considerably more difficult. It is a very rich, clear broth which jells naturally when chilled and is served as a first course either as is or with a variety of garnishes such as boiled eggs, vegetables, caviar, etc. This dish was very popular at elegant dinners in the 1930s when Elizabeth Bowen wrote **The Death of the Heart**. It is seldom made today because it is so difficult and time-consuming. Even Julia Child uses canned.*

JELLIED CONSOMMÉ

Option 1

3	lbs. (at least) of meaty beef, veal, and/or chicken bones
	water to cover the above
1	chopped carrot
1	chopped onion
1/2	cup chopped celery
2	whole cloves
2	teaspoons peppercorns
	salt to taste

Put the bones in a large stockpot and cover them with water. Let them soak for about an hour, then put the pot over a very low heat and cook, barley simmering, for 7 hours.

IMPORTANT: Take great care to see that the pot never comes to a boil, as this will affect the clarity of the broth. Add the remaining ingredients for the last hour of cooking. Remove the bones and strain the broth through a large wire strainer. Chill overnight.

The next day, skim off the solidified fat and discard. Reheat the broth, but again, don't let it boil. Line a large wire strainer with a clean cotton cloth and strain the broth into another container. The result should be a very clear, amber-colored liquid. If it is cloudy, add 1 slightly beaten egg white for every quart of broth and without stirring, very slowly bring it to a simmer and let it cook at this temperature for another 2 hours. Under no circumstances let the broth boil. At the end of 2 hours, strain it once again through cloth as directed above. Chill until jelled and serve.
Yield: Approximately 1 quart

If it does not jell, you can add a package of unflavored gelatin for every quart of broth before rechilling.

OPTION 2:

Buy a can of consommé at the store. Chill and serve.

EMMA

by
Jane Austen

Although *Pride and Prejudice* is Jane Austen's most popular novel, many critics will agree that *Emma* is her best. A grandfather devoted to thin gruel and boiled turnips, an old maid who prattles endlessly about this season's crop of apples, constant rounds of whist, and little suppers of scalloped oysters and minced chicken served next to the fire may not sound like the makings of lively entertainment, but this satire of village life showcases the skill and control of an author in her prime. As with most Jane Austen novels, *Emma* focuses on a few families and their interrelationships, but nineteenth century families were large, so the characters are many, the action intricate, and the comedy high.

The plot, as complicated as a French farce, goes something like this: Emma Woodhouse's friend, Harriet Smith, a poor girl of unknown parentage, has a suitor named Robert Martin, a farmer. But Emma convinces Harriet to turn her affections to Mr. Elton, an eligible young clergyman whom Emma believes loves Harriet, but who actually is in love with Emma. In the meantime, Emma has convinced herself that she and Mr. Churchill—a polished gentleman from out of town—are made for each other, but he, it turns out, is secretly engaged to the elegant and sophisticated Jane Fairfax, whom Emma both dislikes and distrusts. Then Emma loses interest in Mr. Churchill and tries to get her old friend Harriet interested in him instead of in Mr. Elton, who is now involved with a dashing and rich young woman named Augusta Hawkins. But Harriet is by now attracted to Mr. Knightley, Emma's platonic friend and confidant of many years. Emma then discovers that she, herself, is desperately in love with Mr. Knightley, and to her sublime happiness, Knightley returns her love. Harriet is cast aside by them both and is reunited with her original suitor, the simple but honest farmer. Up until now Emma has been greatly devoted to her valetudinarian father, who is reluctant to release her to another's affections, until someone steals a turkey from one of the neighbors, and Mr. Woodhouse decides that with the rising crime rate, they would all be safer with another man in the house, and the book ends with the imminent marriages of just about everybody.

These characters are young, and involved—passively or actively—in the seeking of spouses. Only three—the misses Bates and Emma's father—concern themselves elsewhere. Emma and her father, Mr. Woodhouse, are at the higher end of the village social ladder and as such are central to its social life, which is not exactly dizzying. It consists mainly of family dinners, tea visits, and games of whist. Despite Mr. Woodhouse's irritating pleas for everyone to eat less, sleep more, and stay warm, he is a generous man who shares his largess with the community.

Mrs. and Miss Bates are frequent recipients of his generosity. They are a widow past everything but tea and cards, and her gushing spinster daughter, who prattles on endlessly about anything and everything. Whether it's the behavior of her neighbors or the quality of this season's apples, she "is ever so grateful" and indebted to the kindness of others.

Emma Woodhouse fancies herself a sort of social puppeteer, convinced she knows what's best for everyone, and fully believes that through her machinations she is merely helping fate along. But Emma is mostly wrong, particularly about herself. She is devoted to her aging and foolish father, a man obsessed with the drafts and the dangers of too much exercise, who reveres a dish of thin gruel above all foods, believing as he does in the virtues of a bland diet and quiet living.

Mr. Woodhouse is distressed by large dinner parties, for "His own stomach could bear nothing rich, and he could never believe other people...different..." Although he tries to dissuade all from eating wedding cake at weddings, he feels a very soft boiled egg is not unwholesome, provided it is carefully boiled, a little fresh pork boiled with turnip and carrots a pleasure not to be totally avoided, and an apple—particularly a country apple (well-cooked, of course)—nourishes the body as long as very little exercise is taken. This is only true, however, if the apples and pork come from his own farm and not some faraway and suspect place, but for Mr. Woodhouse, 10 at dinner is a frightening prospect, far too exciting to be good for anyone.

When he donates a loin of pork or recommends an apple for health, Miss Bates soliloquizes endlessly on the deed: on how apples are to be prepared, whether it is better to bake them three times, as Mr. Woodhouse suggests, or to make them into dumplings, on how the pork is to be cooked, (should it be roasted or boiled? Do they have a large enough salting pan?), on how much her niece enjoys apples, on the wisdom of other people, and on how the heavens can look upon her and her poor aging mother so kindly.

While the young people play at intrigues, these three comic characters involve themselves in the small activities that make up village life: trading produce, or putting together a card game with whoever is available. In a larger world than Highbury, people such as Miss Bates and Mr. Woodhouse might be laughed at and rejected, condemned to live lives of loneliness and disconnection, but in a small village this is not so. They may be laughed at, but the community accepts them as they are and finds a place for them in its fold.

Though both Mr. Woodhouse and Miss Bates may be looked upon as foolish, they have compensating characteristics for the community. Mr. Woodhouse, obsessed with health, is not obsessed only with his own, but genuinely cares for the welfare of others, and as the critic A.C. Bradley pointed out, is literature's most perfect gentleman, noticing as he does that Frank Churchill is not thinking of the welfare of others when he leaves doors open to cause a draft.

Miss Bates is overly loquacious and dull, but though she is well past her first youth, she is also an innocent, unassuming, and good-willed woman. Little in the community escapes her undiscerning eye, and she repeats what she has observed without discrimination. It is thus that the attentive listener learns the latest village news in a more pure and objective form than any newspaper could offer. And though Miss Bates is the butt of even public jokes, she has a forgiving nature which should be a model, particularly for the young and often insensitive Emma.

In all of her novels, Jane Austen focuses on a small group of provincial families which, under her probing pen come to stand for the foibles of all humanity. Yet her satire is not the dark variety of a Jonathan Swift; rather, one feels that Austen has true affection for her characters. At the same time that she satirizes them for their foolishness, their vanity, and even their cruelty, she embraces them and accepts them for both their noble and ignoble qualities just as the inhabitants of Highbury learn to accept—even appreciate—the foolish prattlers among them.

000

At Mr. Woodhouse's recommendation, here is the recipe for boiled pork, guaranteed not to cause too much unhealthful excitement. You may add a few herbs, such as bay leaf or rosemary, if you are daring.

VALETUDINARIAN'S BOILED DINNER

1	2 to 3 lbs. pork roast (preferably cut from the leg)
1	carrot, peeled and cut into 6 pieces
1	onion, quartered
1	stalk celery
1	turnip quartered
	a few peppercorns
	water to cover

Bring a kettle of water to a full boil and plunge the roast into it. Bring it to a second boil, skim, and add the remaining ingredients. Cover and simmer 30 minutes for each pound of meat. Remove the roast from the pot and serve with potatoes and cabbage. Save the broth for soup.

SCALLOPED OYSTERS

preheat oven to 350 degrees F.

1	pint oysters
2	cups cracker crumbs
½	cup butter, melted
¾	cup milk
¼	teaspoon salt
¼	teaspoon Worcestershire sauce
	freshly ground black pepper to taste

Drain the oysters, reserving the liquor. Combine the cracker crumbs and butter. Spread 1/3 of the crumbs in a 9-inch pie plate. Cover with half of the oysters. Sprinkle with pepper to taste. Spread another 1/3 of the crumbs on the oysters and cover with the remaining oysters. Add more pepper, if desired. Combine the milk, 1/4 to 1/2 cup of the oyster liquor, salt and Worcestershire sauce. Pour over the assembled dish, and top with the remaining cracker crumbs. Bake at 350 degrees F. for about 40 minutes.
Yield: 4 servings

BAKED APPLES

Although Mr. Woodhouse would have his apples baked three times, once will do it for most tastes.

4	tart apples
¼	cup brown sugar
¼	cup boiling water
	butter

Core the apples and fill them with the sugar. Dot the top of each with butter. Put them in a baking dish and add the boiling water. Cover and bake for about an hour. Serve hot, chilled, or at room temperature.
Yield: 4 servings

APPLE DUMPLINGS

These steamed apple dumplings are from an English recipe circa 1787. They are rather soggy, and modern appetites might prefer them baked rather than steamed.

4 apples

sugar, orange marmalade, or quince jelly

cheesecloth

Enough dough for single crust pie

Core the apples and fill with the sugar and marmalade or jelly. Divide the pie dough into four equal portions and wrap each apple completely in the dough.

Wrap each in a double thickness of cheesecloth and tie securely. Set on a rack in a steamer and steam for 1 to 1-1/2 hours, or until the apples "give" slightly to the touch. Unwrap and serve hot with melted butter or light cream.

You may also bake the apples at 375 degrees F. for about 35 minutes. Baking time will vary with the size of the apples.
Yield: 4 servings

HERZOG

by
Saul Bellow

Saul Bellow's masterpiece, *Herzog*, is a study of a man beset by 1950s urban angst after a disastrous marriage has left him drowning in a sea of his own rhetoric. As his tale begins, Herzog is lunching on the leavings of rats: a half-gnawed loaf of cheap white bread spread with rat molested preserves, canned beans, and American cheese. A man "normally particular about his food" is sharing lovingly with his rodent companions in a dilapidated country house. Food continues to mark Herzog's journey, and the book ends where it begins—with a meal. In the final pages of the novel, Moses Herzog, renewed and at peace, prepares a thank-you dinner of swordfish and spring-chilled wine for the exotic Ramona, at whose table he began to regenerate after his devastating marriage to the beautiful, calculating Madeleine.

The divorce from Madeleine has left him feeling sexually powerless. His beautiful and willful wife lived in a perpetual fantasy that captivated Herzog. Her Catholic convert guilt, her thick woolen suits smudged with make-up, and the heavy cross around her neck inflame Herzog's passion, and Madeleine and Herzog, both born and raised Jews, breed a guilty, self-destructive love.

Throughout the book, Madeleine and Ramona—Herzog's Argentinian mistress, vie for control of Herzog's psyche like warring goddesses. Ramona, a florist by trade, represents the pleasure life still holds out to Herzog: sex, good food, and beautiful surroundings. She wears black lace undergarments and stockings, and high heels that click their way through their owner's fantasy of *La navaja en la liga* (the knife in the garter). Ramona is a Latin lover from Buenos Aires, and she intoxicates with her style: "She entered a room provocatively, swaggering slightly, one hand touching her thigh, as though she carried a knife in her garter belt…. Moses, suffering, suffered in style."

Until Ramona seduces him with her shrimp Arnaud, the intellectual Herzog has been locked into the world of ideas, a prisoner of his own intellectuality, unable to fully experience daily life for the analyzing of it. But the fine food: the melon with prosciutto, the shrimp and rice, and watercress salad, followed by rum-flavored ice cream, brie, biscuits, plums, early green grapes with the brandy and coffee; the table arrangement of spiked red gladiolas; and Ramona's ritual of undressing to reveal her black lace undergarments revitalize him, and thereafter he begins more and more to live life without the constant need to analyze it—to eat, to make love, to walk in the fresh air simply for the sensual pleasure those things give.

Ramona's dinner has an aphrodisiac effect on Herzog and literally transforms him from a man who compulsively analyzes life to a man who experiences life. Aphrodisiacs are a myth as old as sexuality. Oysters, hard boiled eggs, and other foods have historically had aphrodisiac qualities ascribed to them, but the power of the aphrodisiac may lie in the mind: the most susceptible erogenous zone.

Although food probably does not in itself produce sexual stimulation, the wholehearted enjoyment of food can open one to other sensual experiences, such as sex. If you can give yourself to food, you can give yourself to love. If you can give yourself to love, you can give yourself to life. It is no accident that the French are equally famous for their ability to make love and their ability to enjoy good food.

000

Shrimp, Ramona's main course, is a legendary aphrodisiac, as is celery, a main ingredient of this recipe, which eighteenth-century wives used to keep their husbands at home. Both of the following dishes originated at the famed Arnaud's restaurant in New Orleans. Keep in mind that Ramona's dinner takes place way back when sex was still wicked and cholesterol didn't exist. The salad is especially good served after the piquant shrimp Arnaud.

SHRIMP ARNAUD

2	lbs. medium shrimp, cleaned and peeled
¼	cup minced celery
¼	cup minced shallots
¼	cup minced parsley
½	cup prepared mustard
½	cup vinegar
½	cup olive oil
4	minced dried chili peppers (about 1 tsp)
	salt to taste

Combine everything except the shrimp and let stand for ten minutes or so while you boil or steam the shrimp until just done, or until they turn pink, about 10 minutes. Do not overcook or they will toughen. Pour the sauce over the cooked shrimp and toss. Let stand about 15 minutes before serving.
Yield: 4 servings

WATERCRESS SALAD

1	bunch watercress
4	ounces cream cheese
1	tablespoon olive oil

1   tablespoon tarragon white wine vinegar

    salt and freshly ground black pepper to taste

Wash the watercress and pat it dry. Chill. Cream half of the cream cheese with all the other ingredients, then add the chilled watercress. Cut the remaining cream cheese into small pieces, add to the salad, and toss gently with forks.
Yield: 4 servings

THE HOUSE OF MIRTH

by

Edith Wharton

A year after Lily Bart made her debut in society under "a thundercloud of bills," her father told his wife and daughter, hysterical laughter welling up inside him, that they were broke. The conversation took place in the family dining room, where Lily and her mother had just been discussing the possibility of ordering daily fresh flowers for the luncheon table. They were nibbling at the *chaufroix* of the previous night's dinner. It was one of Mrs. Bart's few economies to serve leftovers at luncheon, as long as they were dining *en famile*. Afterall, one serves the finest food not for the pleasure of eating it, but to give the appearance of affluence and sophistication. As for the flowers, Mrs. Bart couldn't have cared less how the room looked when there were no guests present.

Mrs. Bart lived as if she were much richer than she was, putting on a fashionable display for the outside world while her husband struggled to keep her in style. And while one might make little economies in the privacy of the family, "whatever it cost," she always said, "one must have a good cook" and always be what she called "decently dressed," in order to hold one's place in society. Mrs. Bart was what used to be called a "social climber", and she trained her daughter to be that other outdated term: a "gold-digger."

Lily's parents, in Edith Wharton's 1905 novel *The House of Mirth*, both die within a few years of the family's financial ruin, and Lily is thrown upon the only world she knows—the New York upper class—without sufficient funds to maintain herself. She becomes a professional guest of the professional hostesses that swarm around the mansions built by the newly rich "mercantile aristocracy" at the turn of the century.

In the early 1900s, before the federal income tax, before the SEC even, wealthy men were made and destroyed at an accelerated speed, in keeping with the overall quickening of the pace of life brought on by the new motorcars, more and more of which were seen on the city's streets. Tradition and "old money" were losing their primacy in the social order, being replaced by people of unknown origins catapulted by their investments to the huge, sometimes garish Fifth Avenue mansions of other *nouveau riches.*

These "invaders from the west," as Edith Wharton calls them in another novel, brought their wives with them, whom Wharton describes as looking like "jeweler's windows lit by electricity," while the husbands are "carnivorous" and "prey upon" their food. It was the women's job to spend the money these new aristocrats accumulated on the latest fashions, the biggest houses, and the most lavish parties. These women created a world in which a raised eyebrow or the flick of a wicked tongue meant social life or death. While the businessmen speculated with dollars as the medium of exchange, the women dealt in gossip. Just as fortunes hung in the balance on stock market tips, social reputations rose and fell by rumor: Who was seen coming out of whose flat or in the company of whose husband? and when the invitations began to dry up you knew you were in trouble.

A woman was in a particularly difficult position because if she had no income of her own, she must marry one, and that fact sometimes meant liaisons of convenience, rather than love. As Lily Bart puts it, "...a woman is asked out as much for her clothes as for herself.... We are expected to be pretty and well-dressed until we drop, and if we can't keep it up alone, we have to go into partnership."

Lily is by now an expert on the subject. She is 29 years old and has been on the marriage market for a long time; so long, in fact, that she declines serving as a bridesmaid at her cousin Jack Stepney's wedding lest she be too often seen in that role and thereby stimulate undesirable conversations behind her back.

Gertie Farish, on the other hand, while she also has only a small income, has managed to make herself independent of the marriage trade. Like a growing number of women at the time, Gertie lives alone in a small apartment. And although Lily flees to Gertie for comfort after she is ostracized from New York society, she despises the life her friend must lead because she allows the size of her income to dictate her way of living. Gertie has cheap furnishings, no maid, and gushes over the luxuries of others, though without envy. At the Stepney wedding she comments enthusiastically to Lily on the gift display, the dress of the other guests, even the food, in a most common manner: "I always say no one does things better than cousin Grace! Did you ever taste anything more delicious than that mousse of lobster with champagne sauce"? Lily shudders at the gaucheness of the comment. The upper classes, after all, do not notice the delicacies they eat.

Eventually, Lily is down to two marriage choices: Simon Rosedale, an obsequious up-and-comer who has a great deal of money, but who has no personal scruples and will do what he must do to get ahead socially, and Lawrence Selden who, though he has little money, does have personal integrity and loves Lily for all she could be. Thus we see in this society that it is not possible to have both personal integrity and money. One must choose between them.

To Lily's credit, she has difficulty making the choice, but by the time she chooses Rosedale's money it is too late. In her thirst for the life that more money could buy, she has inadvertently compromised herself and the wagging tongues have done their job. Even as eager an outsider as Rosedale is, he will not accept a woman who, it is said, gets "too close" to other women's husbands.

The invitations soon dry up completely. The gossip has cost Lily her hoped-for inheritance from an aging aunt and she is forced into working for her living. Still, Lily persists in her quest to be accepted into society. Lunching on her expectations, she shows herself at restaurants frequented by her old friends, hoping for an accidental meeting which might lead to readmittance. She drags the faithful Gertie Farish with her on these fishing expeditions, and one day, after another much-too expensive lunch, as they are trying to decide between *coupe Jacques* and *peaches a la Melba* for dessert, Lily does find herself face-to-face with one of the major hostesses and a former close friend. The woman gushes affirmations of pleasure at seeing Lily, but in a code that is unmistakable to all within earshot, including the waiters, does not enquire into Lily's future plans or express a desire to see her again. This, then, is the final signal that Lily Bart's career as a professional guest is over.

000

The food of the rich in 1900 was just that—rich. Besides being pre-income tax, the period was also pre-cholesterol. Most of the following recipes are high in fat, as well as cost.

SALMON CHAUD-FROID

Chaud-froid sauce is actually more a "frosting" for cold meats than a sauce, as we usually employ the term today. Originally, it was made by boiling the knuckles of the feet of calves to get a jelly, but most cooks, including Julia Child, now use unflavored gelatin instead. This sauce can be used to cover all sorts of cold fish, eggs, and poultry for buffet service. The first layer, opaque, holds in place the decorations made of truffles, pimiento, or vegetables, and the second layer, which is clear, covers the decorations and makes them glisten. You can chill the leftover clear jelly until firm, chop it, and surround the dish with it. It catches the light and shimmers beautifully.

Be sure to skin the fish or poultry before covering with the gelatin mixtures. Although the following recipe uses salmon, any fish or poultry may be substituted.

1   whole salmon

3   envelopes unflavored gelatin

2   cups sour cream

4   cups clear chicken broth

         steamed vegetables for decoration

Poach the salmon, chill, and remove the skin. Dissolve the gelatin in the broth and divide the mixture into two equal portions. Beat the sour cream into 2 cups of the broth. Set the bowl in a larger one that has been filled with cracked ice, and stir the mixture until it is slightly thickened. Put the fish on a large piece of waxed paper. Spoon the sour cream mixture over the fish, covering all exposed surfaces. Decorate with the vegetables as you wish. Refrigerate both the fish and the reserved clear mixture. When the clear mixture is thick but not completely set, spoon it over the fish, covering the entire exposed surface. Chill until serving time. Remove the waxed paper and transfer the completed Chaud-froid to a platter.

LOBSTER MOUSSE

Any fin or shellfish, cooked or uncooked, can be used in place of the lobster for mousse with champagne sauce, in the following recipe.

Preheat oven to 350 degrees.

2	cups cooked lobster
1½	tablespoons butter
1	tablespoon flour
¼	cup milk
2	eggs, separated
¼	teaspoon salt
1	cup heavy cream
	pinch of paprika

Grind the lobster, using a food processor or blender. Melt the butter in a small saucepan. While over heat, blend in the flour with the butter. Stir the milk into the mixture and maintain the heat until the mixture thickens slightly. Remove from the heat, and whisk in the egg yolks. Add the salt and paprika. Stir thoroughly, and add the ground lobster. Whip the egg whites and the cream into this mixture. Lightly grease an attractive baking dish and pour the mixture into it. Set the baking dish in a larger pan of hot water. Put it into the oven and bake for about 40 minutes.

CHAMPAGNE SAUCE

2	tablespoons butter
2	cups sliced mushrooms
2	tablespoons flour
1	cup champagne

1	cup half and half
1	tablespoon brandy

Melt the butter in a heavy skillet, and sauté the mushrooms until limp. Add the flour, and blend. Pour in the Champagne, stir, and boil until the liquid is reduced by at least half. Add the half and half, a small amount at a time, stirring, until the sauce is the consistency you desire. (It may not be necessary to use all the half and half.)
Stir in the brandy and serve with the mousse.
Yield: 4 servings

PEACHES À LA MELBA

2	large fresh peaches
1	cup granulated sugar
1	cup water
¼	teaspoon vanilla
1	cup fresh raspberries, puréed
	vanilla ice cream

Peel, halve and pit the peaches. Put the sugar and water in a saucepan and stir until the sugar is dissolved. Bring to a boil over medium heat for five minutes, add the vanilla and the peach halves, and simmer until tender. Chill. Line four dessert glasses with as much vanilla ice cream as desired. Top each with a peach half and surround it with the raspberry purée.
Yield: 4 servings

The following dessert is traditionally served only in silver or crystal dessert cups or glasses. Although the technical difference between an ice and a sorbet may have to do with the addition of egg whites, the terms are interchangeable in commercial products. Sherbet is a possible substitute, although it lacks the tartness of sorbet or ice.

COUPE JACQUES

1	cup diced fresh pineapple
1	cup sliced bananas
1	cup dark cherries, halved and pitted
1	cup strawberries, halved
2	cups kirsch
1	tablespoon grenadine syrup
	fruit ice or sorbet

Mix together the fruits and cover them with the kirsch. Add the grenadine syrup, and allow to macerate for an hour. When ready to serve, put a spoonful of fruit in the bottom of a dessert glass and top with a scoop of fruit ice. Decorate, if desired, with a sprig of fresh mint.

Yield: 6 servings

INVISIBLE MAN

by
Ralph Ellison

In a country that values individualism above all else, the search for identity takes us far beyond geography, class, and race, and our common search brings us closer together than societal differences can ever separate us. Ralph Ellison's classic novel on the search for identity, *Invisible Man*, is not only a story of a descendant of slaves trying to break away from his past and his people's history and find his place in the wider culture, it is also the story of all Americans, struggling for identity in a society that allows class mobility and invites endless reinvention of the self, the sloughing off of the past, and the donning of the new. As James Baldwin points out in *Nobody Knows My Name*, the black American experience and the white American experience reveal the same things about society: "I didn't meet anyone in that [white] world who didn't suffer from the very same affliction that all the people I had fled from suffered from and that was that they didn't know who they were."

The unnamed narrator of *Invisible Man* begins his journey to self-acceptance in the often anthologized "Battle Royal" scenes where he is forced to endure, among several humiliating pranks of the white men, drunken jeers as he recites his high school valedictorian speech, competing with the undulating body of a white woman for the attention of the crowd. In spite of this, he is given a full scholarship to a small, all black college for his trouble, and spends the next three years determined to be "a credit to his race." In traditional Horatio Alger fashion, he studies hard, keeps regular hours, is attentive at chapel, scrupulously deodorizes his body so as not to give offense, and keeps his goal clearly in mind—to be asked to stay on after graduation as a teacher or administrator, never realizing that he has accepted for himself a persona created by whites of the best a black man can be. The scholarship can be no more than a ticket further into his separate world and an ever-present debt to the white community. Ellison exposes this hoax of false hope when in a dream the narrator opens his briefcase to find not the white man's scholarship, but a piece of paper with the directive, "Keep This Nigger-Boy Running."

Ironically, it is the president of the college, Dr. Bledsoe, who deceives the young man into his flight north, to Harlem, where he finds his dreams suddenly and cruelly shattered, and with them the understanding of who he is and his place in the world. Headed north on the bus for New York, armed with the still-gleaming leather briefcase given to him by the white men at the Battle Royal, and with what he thinks are letters of recommendation to New York's rich and powerful, the narrator looks forward to the summer, and to returning to college in the fall a wiser and more sophisticated man. However, unbeknown to him, his idol, Dr. Bledsoe has sabotaged his academic career. In response to the narrator's foolish error of showing the wrong side of the black community to a white trustee, the letters actually contain an indictment of his character and inform the addressee that under no circumstances will the young man be allowed back into the school.

When he finally finds out the truth, the narrator's rage is overwhelming. He imagines himself attacking the falsely humble Bledsoe with a rope of raw, unclean chitterlings, sticky and dripping. "Bledsoe," he might say, "...you're a shameless chitterling eater. I accuse you of relishing hog bowels...I accuse you of indulging in a filthy habit." For all his life, Bledsoe has tried to deny his heritage and has made for himself a personal power-base at the college by taking up what he perceives to be the more refined ways of the white society and ingratiating himself with the white community, withstanding his own humiliation at the hands of white men. All the while he repudiates the culture that bore and bred him, withholds himself from his weaker brothers, and sacrifices his own for a taste of the white world. The hog's bowels the narrator imagines lugging out for all the world to see is the diet of the underclass—a diet of shame that both Bledsoe and he wish to deny in themselves.

Like Dr. Bledsoe, this young student feels embarrassment at his cultural background. When he first arrives in Harlem, he lies back on his bed at Men's House, full of blind hope and innocent optimism, and dreams of being like the men he saw in *Esquire* magazine—suave, soft-spoken, and elegant—and he decides to reinvent himself as a northerner, to slough off his southern ways, and to return to college in the fall, having risen above his origins. But he finds it more difficult to convince others of his northern identity. He needs to only walk into a drug store cafe to be immediately identified by the counterman, who offers him a southern breakfast of pork chops, grits, eggs, hot biscuits and coffee. Insulted, the new urbanite coldly orders orange juice, toast, and coffee in an attempt to convince others, as well as himself, that he is someone other than who he is.

Shortly after his fantasy of exposing Dr. Bledsoe's chitterling-eating past, the narrator walks downtown past a clutter of small businesses, barber shops, fish houses, beauty parlors, and hog maw joints, and is affronted by an advertisement for skin whitener: "You too can be truly beautiful. Win greater happiness with a whiter complexion. Be outstanding in your social set." Resisting an urge to smash his hand through the window, he rushes on through the icy wind toward the warming fire of a man selling fresh-baked yams and is seized with nostalgia as the sweet smell wafts his direction. "At home we'd bake them in the hot coals of the fireplace, had carried them cold to school for lunch; munched them secretly, squeezing the pulp from the soft peel...we'd loved them candied or baked in a cobbler, deep-fat fried in a pocket of dough, or roasted with pork and glazed with the well-browned fat."

He buys one and bites into it, its skin bursting with juices, its sweet pulp running with melted butter, and succumbs to a wave of home-sickness, ubt he is also momentarily aware of his embarrassment at loving so much a symbol of the black south. Yams, like hog maw and the chitterlings he just a moment ago had dreamed of hurling in the face of Dr. Bledsoe are a sign of their mutual heritage which until now the narrator has sought to disclaim. But the primitive vision of attacking Dr. Bledsoe with the dripping organ has purged him of his shame at being a black and a southerner, for he runs back to the old yam seller.

To hell with being ashamed of what you liked, he thought. *No more of that for me.* He buys two more and devours them on the spot.

"I can see you one of these old-fashioned yam eaters," the old man comments. "They're my birthmark," the narrator replies. "I yam what I yam."

000

Dr. George Washington Carver, the distinguished agricultural researcher, brought the yam to prominence in the South. He persuaded farmers to plant this highly nutritious tuber as an alternative to the soil-depleting cotton. Yams come in many varieties, all of which are interchangeable in recipes, and are very high in vitamin A. They spoil easily, however, so buy only as many as you will use at one time.

FRIED YAM PIES

*The young narrator of **Invisible Man** fondly remembers them deep fried in a pocket of dough, which is undoubtedly a reference to the fried pie, one of the most delectable of southern desserts.*

The yams for the filling can be either baked or boiled. Have them ready before you start the pastry.
Pastry:

2	cups flour, sifted
1	teaspoon baking soda
½	cup vegetable shortening
	ice water
	fat for frying

Sift the dry ingredients together into a mixing bowl. Cut in the shortening. Sprinkle the ice water over the dough a tablespoon at a time, mixing lightly, until the dough can be shaped into a ball. Roll out the dough and cut it into rounds with a large cookie cutter.

Filling:

1	cup cooked yams, mashed
1/3	cup brown sugar
½	teaspoon ground cinnamon
¼	teaspoon ground nutmeg

1/8   teaspoon ground ginger

1/8   teaspoon ground cloves

Combine ingredients thoroughly. Put a small amount on each pastry round. The amount will depend on the size of the rounds. Fold the dough over the filling and seal the edge with a fork. (Wetting the edge slightly with water will help seal it tighter.) Fry in deep hot fat until golden brown on both sides. Drain on paper towels. Yield: 4 pies

YAM COBBLER

A cousin of the sweet potato pie and a variation on the fruit cobbler, yam cobbler is a wholesome, if heavy, dessert. This cobbler is a casual affair. It can be baked in a deep casserole dish or a shallow baking pan.

Filling:

2   lbs. yams, boiled, peeled and sliced

1   cup brown sugar

4   tablespoons butter

Dough:

1   cup flour

1¼   teaspoons baking powder

2   tablespoons soft butter

½   cup milk

Put the yams in a small baking dish, spread the sugar over them, and dot with the 4 tablespoons of butter. Combine the remaining ingredients thoroughly and drop the dough by spoonfuls over the tops of the yams. Bake until nicely browned in a 400 degree F oven Yield: 1 cobbler

CANDIED YAMS

We're all familiar with the sticky marshmallow-covered mass that tastes more of sugar than yams served at many Thanksgiving dinners. But this simple southern treat highlights the flavor of the yams instead of overwhelming it.

6   medium yams, cooked, peeled and sliced

1/3   cup butter

2/3   cup brown sugar

¼   teaspoon salt

1/3   cup water

In a heavy skillet, heat together the butter and brown sugar, stirring until melted and blended and a syrup has formed. Add the sweet potatoes, turning them in the syrup until coated. Add the salt and water, cover and cook on low heat for a few minutes until the water is absorbed.
Yield: 10 servings

PORK ROAST WITH YAMS

Also traditionally cooked with roasted opossum, yams particularly complement a pork roast. Just add them, peeled and quartered, to the roasting pan for the last hour or so, basting them frequently with the pan juices.

BAKED YAMS

Plain baked yams dripping with melted butter, the way the street vendor cooks them, are marvelous. You can do them as the narrator remembers, buried in hot coals, wrapped in aluminum foil or not. Cooking time will vary a great deal. Check them after 40 minutes, and every 20 minutes thereafter. They should give easily when the skin is lightly pressed. You can also bake them in a conventional oven or microwave, as you would white potatoes. Serve split, with a chunk of butter.
Yield: 1 yam per serving

JANE EYRE

by
Charlotte Brontë

Charlotte Brontë's *Jane Eyre* has long been thought of as the prototype for the feminine gothic romance; it features a feisty heroine who must make her own way in the world, mysterious midnight occurrences in isolated country estates, and dark and brooding heroes. The book was an instant bestseller at its publication in 1847, and has remained popular ever since.

Jane Eyre was a new model of heroine, an innovative addition to the literary canon of the time. She is intelligent, assertive, plain in appearance, and independent. As a ten-year-old living with her Aunt Reed, Jane resists the insults and physical attacks of her cousins, hurling return epithets and right uppercuts to the jaw with the best of them. She is unfailingly forthright and unequivocating in her speech, does not pretend to like those she despises, and speaks her mind to all who question her. She neither exaggerates nor denigrates her intellectual accomplishments, but looks at herself and the world honestly and realistically. Long thought of as a feminine novel, *Jane Eyre* is actually an early feminist novel.

Orphaned in babyhood, Jane lives with a cruel aunt who treats her as a servant to the other children and separates her from the family circle, even at Christmas. When Jane is ten her aunt sends her to Lowood Institution, a boarding school for orphaned girls. There Jane endures tremendous hardship at the hands of the tyrannical and tight-fisted headmaster, Mr. Brocklehurst. The girls are subjected to harsh discipline, long hours of prayer, freezing rooms, and subsistence rations. After rising before dawn and washing in ice-crusted water, followed by an hour or so of prayer, they are fed burned porridge for breakfast. Dinner is a rancid concoction of "rusty" meat and potatoes, and five o'clock tea a half slice of bread each and a swallow of coffee. This is followed by the evening meal: a torn-off bit of oatcake and water drunk from a common cup. Because of their poor living conditions, most of the Lowood girls eventually succumb to an epidemic and Jane, a survivor in all ways, stays on. Later, as one of Lowood's success stories, she becomes a teacher there for a short time.

As a grown woman, Jane becomes bored with the limited life she has led and takes a job as a governess at Thornfield Hall, 70 miles away from Lowood. There she falls in love with her employer, the handsome but melancholy Mr. Rochester, only to find out before the wedding that the eerie midnight visitations, the chilling wails, and other assorted mischief are not the products of either of an overworked imagination or poltergeists, but of a madwoman who lives in the attic of the old manse—none other than the first Mrs. Rochester, alive but decidedly unwell.

This means, of course, that Jane cannot legally be Mr. Rochester's wife. She refuses to be his mistress, and despite his passionate pleas, Jane leaves him and sets out once again, alone and undercapitalized, to make a place for herself in the world. This time, before she manages to find another position, complete with another suitor, she is reduced to actually begging for food along the roadside. Wandering in a strange village like "a lost and starving dog," she importunes a farmer for a piece of his dinner and uses her hands to eat the cold, congealed porridge that had been rejected by the pigs.

In the end, Thornfield Hall burns to the ground with Mrs. Rochester in it, and after more trials and travails, Jane and Mr. Rochester finally wed. His marriage of the virtuous and the profane became the stuff of romantic fiction for the next 150 years, but Jane Eyre would not have endured so long had it been only a potboiler.

In a time when it was thought delightfully feminine to be indirect, Jane says to Rochester in an early conversation, "I don't think, sir, you have the right to command me merely because you are older than I or because you have seen more of the world than I have; your claim to superiority depends on the use you have made of your time and experience." Rochester falls in love with, Jane not for her feminine dress and appearance, for Jane's hair is straight and her clothing starkly plain; not for her feminine wiles, for, by her own description her smile is neither complacent nor submissive and she is a plainspoken person, who values character above all else, but because of her strong character, her independent nature, and her candor. Rochester's first physical impulse toward Jane is not a fatherly pat of affection nor a kiss of passion, both of which might have been expected in 1847, but a decidedly unexpected desire for a firm handshake. Jane Eyre was one of the first women in literature to be respected as an equal by her suitor.

Although conditions at Lowood may seem exaggerated and melodramatic, they have a basis in Charlotte Brontë's own experience. After his wife's death, Reverend Brontë sent his daughters Charlotte and Emily (author of *Wuthering Heights*) to a school for the children of impoverished ministers. The school later became Charlotte's model for Lowood Institution, and by all accounts her rendering is accurate. There, students were so poorly fed that typhus and consumption ravaged the populace, and Charlotte and Emily nearly died before their father removed them.

000

Oatmeal is the basis of the Lowood orphan's diet. Charlotte Brontë was born in and grew up in Yorkshire, in the north of England, where the food would likely be influenced by Scotland. Porridge is a mainstay, and is treated with considerable reverence. Many families used to keep a special pot to be used for porridge only, just as many Italian families still keep a special pan for polenta. Traditionally, porridge is stirred with a kind of wooden spoon called a "spurtle," a "theevil," or in Shetland, a "gruel-tree."

PORRIDGE

To make a classic porridge, allow a scant cup of water (spring water or filtered water if possible) and about 1/2 cup of oatmeal for each serving. Bring the water to a boil and add the oatmeal in a steady stream while stirring briskly. Cover and let cook at very low heat for about 20 minutes. Add a pinch of salt for each serving, stir, and serve with cream, milk, or buttermilk. Those with American tastes might want to add some brown sugar with the milk. Although more glutinous than what you might be accustomed to, this has a nice flavor.

ORPHAN OATCAKE LOWOOD

Oatcakes are actually quite tasty when heated and served with jam. Mixing the dough in a food processor with the metal blade makes the dough easy to work with. Other methods are likely to result in a far less desirable texture.

2	cups dry oatmeal
4	teaspoons vegetable oil
1	teaspoon salt
2	cups warm water (you will probably need less than the entire 2 cups)

Mix all ingredients by hand with just enough water to moisten. Put the mixture into a food processor, using the metal blade. Process only a few seconds, until the dough forms a ball. Roll out on a floured surface to about the thickness of a pie crust, cut into 4 triangles, and cook on the top of the stove on a hot griddle or frying pan until firm.
Re-heat in the oven and serve with jam.
Yield: 4 oatcakes

WELSH RABBIT

Young Jane is unhappy with the food at her Aunt Reed's house, but after a few meals at Lowood, the nursery staple of Welsh Rabbit and baked whole onions seems like a feast. Welsh rabbit is not rabbit at all, but a cheese sauce served over toast. It was reportedly served for dinner when hunters came home empty-handed. It makes a very tasty late supper.

2	cups sharp cheddar cheese, shredded
¾	cup milk
1	teaspoon dry mustard
1	teaspoon Worcestershire sauce
	dash cayenne
1	beaten egg
	prepared horseradish or mustard

In a heavy saucepan heat the cheese and milk over low heat, stirring constantly until the cheese melts. Add the dry mustard, Worcestershire sauce and cayenne. Stir a bit of this mixture into the beaten egg, and return all to the saucepan. Continue to cook and stir over low heat until the mixture thickens. Serve over toast spread with horseradish sauce or prepared mustard, according to taste. Serve with baked onions.

BAKED WHOLE ONIONS

Preheat oven to 375 degrees F.

Wash whole unpeeled onions, put them in a buttered baking dish, and bake until tender, about 1 hour. Don't be shocked at their charred appearance. Simply slice of the root end, squeeze out the steaming centers and discard the rest. Yield: 4 servings

HOT NEGUS

When Jane finally leaves Lowood for her first job, it is a coach ride of 18 hours in the bitter cold. Upon her arrival at Thornfield Hall, the housekeeper brings her sand-

wiches and hot negus, an excellent warming drink to serve in front of a winter fire, but also refreshing when served cooled.

1	cup ruby port
2	teaspoons sugar
2	cups hot water
	nutmeg

Dissolve the sugar in the port, add hot water, and stir. Pour into mugs and grate some nutmeg on top.
Yield: 2 servings

SEED CAKE

Even those in charge at Lowood have difficulty filling their stomachs. Miss Temple, a kindly teacher, has Jane and her friend Helen to tea in her room and can't even get an extra piece of toast from the kitchen for them to share. But saving the day, she pulls a large seed cake from her private cupboard and the three blissfully share it. This is a popular tea cake in Britain. The seeds are caraway, and they add a surprisingly pleasant flavor.

Preheat oven to 350 degrees.

½	pound softened butter
4	eggs
1 ½	cups sugar
3	cups sifted flour
3	teaspoons baking powder
¾	cup milk
	juice and rind of 1 lemon
1	tablespoon vanilla
2	teaspoons caraway seeds

Butter a bundt cake pan and dust it with flour. Cream softened butter and slowly stir in sugar. Add eggs one at a time and beat until the mixture is a light lemon color. Stir in the lemon juice, rind, and vanilla. Mix the sifted flour, baking powder, and caraway seeds and add to the creamed mixture alternating with the milk. Begin and end with the flour. Pour the batter into the pan and bake for about 1 hour, or until it tests done. Remove from the oven and cool in the pan for 15 minutes.

LOVE IN THE TIME OF CHOLERA

by
Gabriel García Márquez

"Delirious with joy" after receiving the first of his beloved's letters, Florentino Ariza spent the afternoon "eating roses and reading the note letter by letter, over and over again, and the more he read the more roses he ate…"

It was Florentino's seventeenth year and he had fallen into devastating love, with a passion that never faltered and which defined all facets of his life therafter until the consummation of his love, more than fifty years later.

Love in the Time of Cholera, by the Latin-American master Gabriel García Márquez, is an epic story of love, celebrating sensuosity in all its forms. The old unnamed Caribbean city in which the story takes place is a city of fine homes and lush with flowers of delicate beauty and perfume. Their sweetness mingles with the fetid odors of the sewage-laden river—source of cholera, with its symptoms of the malady of love—and along the waterfront it mingles with the cloying sweetness of cheap perfume.

The various social classes of the town mix at wharfside establishments over fried mullets, coconut rice, and Jamaican punch, and at the transient hotel frequented by "little night birds" who sell "emergency love." It is here, in this hotel, among these women, that Florentino Ariza spends so many hours in blissful suffering over Fermina Daza, his first—and last—love. In the beginning he takes a room only so he can have a place in which to read romantic poetry and feverishly compose his own verses. Florentino Ariza has the soul of a poet, but the pen of a sentimental romantic. So love-soaked is his writing that even his business correspondence reeks of passion. His bills of lading rhyme, and the lyrical spirit of his memos diminishes their authority.

Over time he becomes a sort of pet of the prostitutes, and later, one of their most enthusiastic clients. He stops in nearly every day after work and dines among a bevy of naked nymphs, many of whom carry their history on their bodies in scars: "starbursts of gunshot wounds, ridges of the razor cuts of love. Caesarian sections sewn up by butchers." Each of the women cooks something, and no one eats better than Florentino, for he accepts morsels from each of them.

During the fifty or so years that it takes for the husband of his beloved Fermina Daza to die from the infirmities of old age, Florentino manages to have a total of 622 love affairs, some of them with the "little night birds" and some with women stolen from other men. One of his longest is with Ausencia Santander, a grandmother, and mistress of the riverboat captain Rosendo de la Rosa who with great enthusiasm takes his friend Florentino to meet her. They come to her door, carrying a demijohn of homemade aguardiente and the ingredients "for an epic sancocho, the kind that was possible only with chickens from the patio, meat with tender bones, rubbish-heap pork, and greens and vegetables from the towns along the river."

Before the sancocho is ready, having finished half the demijohn of firewater, the captain passes into a deep slumber, and by the magic of Eros, Florentino and Ausencia instantly begin a secret love that will last for years. They are able to elude the captain because he is an excellent sailor and always notifies the port of his arrival with the ship's horn: "...three long howls for his wife and nine children, and then...two short, melancholy ones for his mistress," the signal for Florentino to put on his clothing and slip out the door.

Meanwhile, Fermina Daza, who was thirteen years old when Florentino was first seized by the ecstatic pangs of love for her, becomes the happy and contented wife of Dr. Juvenal Urbino, one of the most respected men in the community. Although in her early youth Fermina returned her admirer's passion and had even accepted Florentino's proposal of marriage with a note in her still childish hand that said, "Very well, I will marry you if you promise not to make me eat eggplant," by the time she is mature enough for marriage, after years of passionate correspondence with Florentino, she can't stand the sight of him any more than she can bear the flavor of eggplant.

Ironically, Fermina Daza spends the first years of her marriage in the house of a mother-in-law who served eggplant daily in all its forms, but when Doña Blanca Urbino finally dies and Fermina Daza is at last the mistress of her own home, in full command of her life, and having reached full marital harmony, a curious thing happens. She begins to love eggplant: pureed eggplant, stuffed eggplant, eggplant in all its forms, so much so that her husband would joke that he wanted another daughter so he could name her for the beloved vegetable: Eggplant Urbino.

At the time in her life when she begins to love eggplant, Fermina Daza learns the single irrevocable fact of her existence: her life has been leant to her by her husband, and she is his servant. Although he never mistreats her and she remains on the whole a very happy woman, she was freed of the illusions of youth. She doesn't blame him; she blames life. She is in his holy service, and he is a demanding pontiff. At the hint of imperfection in the food, he would push away his plate, saying, "This meal has been prepared without love."

But she learns to love her husband's capricious demands—even loves him because of them—as she learns to love eggplant. He, in turn, comes to accept her unrelenting stubbornness. In the most serious quarrel of their life together, Fermina Daza steadfastly refuses to admit that she has left her husband without bath soap for a week. For four months they dine in steely silence, sleep in separate rooms, rail at one another, and open old wounds and turn them into fresh ones. Finally, beaten into submission by her sheer obstinacy, he capitulates. One night he lies down beside her in the bed that had been in his family for three generations and says, "Let me stay here....There was soap," even though both know that it is not true. She had forgotten to replace it.

When Dr. Urbino—founder of the Medical Society, eradicator of cholera, organizer of the construction of the first aqueduct, President of the Academy of Language, Knight of the Order of the Holy Sepulcher, Commander in the Legion of Honor, and the restorer of the Dramatic Theater—dies from a fall while trying to rescue his Latin-speaking parrot from a Mango tree, the citizens of the town are so grateful for his zealous community-mindedness that they have his portrait painted and display it for several months "in the vast gallery of The Golden Wire, a shop that sold imported merchandise" before hanging it permanently in the School of Fine Arts. The last guest to leave the long series of ceremonies marking the death of the town's leading citizen is Florentino Ariza. He stays not only to present his sincere condolences to the devastated widow, but to pledge his everlasting love to her, as he had done well over 50 years earlier. Florentino Ariza wins back the love of Fermina Daza in his seventy-eighth year and her seventy-fourth. They consummate their love on a boat trip, sailing up and down the river on a seemingly endless voyage of lovemaking, and reveal to us a fundamental secret of life: "...that it is life, more than death, that has no limits."

000

SANCOCHO

Sancocho, the national dish of Columbia, is simply a boiled dinner. It contains few spices other than a lot of garlic and, as Gabriel García Márquez's description implies, is quite dependent for its flavor on the type and quality of meats and vegetables used. You can use any combination of meat, poultry, and vegetables, but ones common to Latin America will, of course, lend more authenticity. For a stronger flavor, add a few spicy sausages to the pot. In case you have no chickens on your patio, as the narrator recommends, you can buy one at the store.

1	chicken, cut up
	several spicy link sausages such as Italian
½	pound lean pork cut into one inch cubes
	about 2 dozen pearl onions, peeled
1	entire head of garlic, peeled
2	tomatoes, chopped
1	medium sweet potato, peeled and sliced
1	lb. yucca, peeled and sliced (available in specialty markets)
1	medium yam, peeled and sliced
3	plantains (available in specialty markets)
1	pound yellow winter squash, peeled and cubed
2	ears of corn, cut into 3 pieces each
1	bunch of tender greens
	salt and pepper to taste

Put the meats, onion, garlic, and tomatoes in a large stock pot, cover with water and bring to a boil. Reduce heat and simmer for two hours. Remove the meats and add all the other ingredients except the plantains, corn and greens and continue simmering until the vegetables are done: 30 to 45 minutes. Meanwhile, boil the plantains, corn, and greens, and return the meats to the pot. Cook another 5 minutes and serve.

Yield: 8 servings

A mainstay of Caribbean menus, coconut rice is a savory version of rice pudding and goes well with any white fish. You can make coconut milk by grating fresh coconut in the food processor and mixing it with a combination of water and the juice drained from the whole coconut. You can also use a handful of dried, unsweetened coconut, steeped in 2 or 3 cups of boiling water for an hour or so. Or even easier, dilute the canned coconut milk with water to desired richness if the canned product is available at specialty food stores in your area.

COCONUT RICE

¼   cup raisins

2 ½   cups coconut milk

1   cup rice

1   teaspoon sugar

Soak the raisins in the coconut milk for about half an hour in a tightly-covered saucepan. Add the rice and sugar. Bring to a boil, then reduce the heat to low and cook until all the liquid has been absorbed, about 30 minutes.
Yield: 4 servings

Eggplant is a very popular dish in Latin American countries, and is served both as a side dish and as a main course. With all the eggplant Fermina Daza cooked in her life, she undoubtedly included the following 2 recipes in her repertoire.

EGGPLANT AND GREEN BEAN SALAD

½   lb. eggplant, peeled and cut into julienne strips

     salt

1   small onion, chopped fine

2   tablespoons vegetable oil

4   medium tomatoes, diced

ground black pepper

1/3   cup pimento-stuffed green olives, sliced

1   cup green beans

1   tablespoon fresh parsley, chopped

2   tablespoons vegetable oil

2   tablespoons vinaigrette

Put the eggplant in a colander, sprinkle with salt, and let stand for about 1/2
hour. Heat the oil in a skillet. Rinse salt from eggplant and drain. Sauté the
onion and eggplant over medium heat until both are soft. Add the tomatoes
and black pepper. Stir in the olives and cook for another 5 minutes. Meanwhile, cook the beans in boiling water until they are tender. Drain, and add
them to the other ingredients. Transfer to a serving bowl, toss with vinaigrette, and cool to room temperature before serving.
Yield: 4 servings

STUFFED EGGPLANT

1   medium eggplant

3   tablespoons vegetable oil

1   small onion, chopped fine

1   cup fresh breadcrumbs

1   cup grated Munster cheese

½   cup chopped ham

1   beaten egg

       salt and pepper

Preheat oven to 375 degrees F.

Cut the eggplant in half lengthwise. Score and cut sides with a sharp knife and sprinkle generously with salt. Let stand for about 30 minutes, then rinse to remove the salt. Remove the center flesh and chop, leaving the two shells for stuffing. Sauté the onion in the oil, add the chopped eggplant and sauté until soft. Remove from the heat. Stir in the breadcrumbs, cheese, ham, egg, and salt and pepper to taste. Divide the mixture evenly between the two shells and bake for about 40 minutes.
Yield: 2 servings

JAMAICAN PUNCH

Jamaican punch is the name given to a large variety of rum drinks mixed with citrus juices. It's the traditional drink of the Caribbean, and is also known as "Planter's Punch." The following is a simple and very refreshing version.

Juice of 2 limes

2 teaspoons powdered sugar

2 ounces plain soda water

2 dashes bitters

2 ounces rum

Mix all the ingredients and serve in a tall glass over shaved ice.
Yield: 1 drink

MADAME BOVARY

by
Gustave Flaubert

Emma Roualt wanted to be married at midnight by the light of torches, but this idea seemed silly to her father. Instead, she and Charles Bovary, her betrothed, led their wedding procession into the village on a bright spring afternoon. The line of celebrants resembles "a single brightly colored scarf undulating across" the Normandy fields. Emma's dress trails through the green grain, picking up an occasional thistle, which she daintily removes, while her new husband stands by helplessly and the fiddler plays with such enthusiasm that he scares away all the birds for miles. A disorderly band of citizens and their children follow the new couple, discussing farm business or "playing tricks on each other's backs, working themselves up in advance for the merriment that was to come."

Meanwhile, a country wedding feast is set up at her father's farm. There are roasts of mutton and beef, six chicken fricassees, veal a la casserole, a beautiful suckling pig dressed out with sausages, quivering yellow custard with the initials of the newlyweds in sugared almonds, and foaming cider and calvados—libations native to the region.

The wedding cake, presented with great flourish, is an extravaganza of porticos and colonnades with stucco and statuettes in niches, sprinkled with gilt paper stars. The second tier is a spongecake castle tower surrounded by bits of angelica, almonds, raisins and orange, and the top layer a pastoral green meadow with jelly lakes, hazelnut shell boats, and a tiny cupid in a chocolate swing.

Altogether the feast lasts 16 hours, the constant eating is interrupted by games of cork-penny, feats of strength, "spicy" stories, and much singing. When it is time to leave, the oat-stuffed horses can only be harnessed with great difficulty by their equally stuffed and merry owners, and all night long there are runaway carryalls bouncing along the country roads and sideswiping embankments. Those who stay over spend the night in the kitchen drinking hot toddies made with kirsch, an impromptu combination thought up by the father of the bride. At dawn they send to Saint-Victor for more cigars, and they start all over again. It goes on like this for several more days, even after the bride and groom leave for their new home.

As the new wife of Dr. Charles Bovary, Emma is an instant success, carrying out her domestic duties with a style that befits the wife of the town's only physician. She always manages an attractive meal for their dinner guests, composed from the exquisite meat, fruit, and dairy products of the Normandy region in which they live. She writes little notes to his patients, reminding them of what they owe, but managing to make them sound like personal greetings instead of requests for payment. She even turns the jelly from its jar onto a pretty dish before serving. It turns out, however, that these are not the habits of an accomplished housewife, but the airs of a woman who aspires far beyond her circumstances.

Emma soon grows tired of the dull middle-class life they lead and begins to lose herself in romantic novels and daydreams of luxurious surroundings and passionate suitors. She feels contempt for her husband, so far from the courtly ideal she dreams of. Her daily life seems paltry compared to that of La Vaubyessard, the local chateau where she and Charles are invited to attend a grand ball. This fete is to become the highlight of Emma's short life.

The chateau is a large Italianate residence with three front entrances, an immense lawn, and legions of servants. Ladies and gentlemen amuse themselves at billiards and idle chatter, and the well-fitted portrait gallery attests to a long tradition of this way of life. At dinner, the fragrance of flowers and fine linen mingle, the cut glass and silver gleam, and not all of the ladies tuck their gloves into their wine glasses by way of refusing a drink. Emma tastes champagne for the first time, and its creamy coldness causes her to shiver delightedly. When the air in the ballroom becomes stuffy, a servant nonchalantly breaks out two of the windowpanes and the dancing continues. In a memorable tableau from the ball, Flaubert catches Emma surrounded by the soft candlelight, aswoon from the music. Tasting a little silver shell of Maraschino ice with eyes half shut, she has given herself to the moment completely, almost doubting that her other life exists.

What Emma does not realize is that she and her husband were only invited by the Marquis as a condescending gesture to simple, middle class people who have done him a favor, and that the invitation was issued only after reflecting on whether or not they could be counted on to blend in with the other guests and not make a fool of their host with their rustic ways.

Emma becomes deeply depressed after her exposure to such glamour. Back in her own modest dining room, over a typical Normandy meal of veal with sorrel, she looks upon her husband and the life they lead with scorn. Emma Bovary is a woman of many delusions. Not only does she feel that her life should be filled with beauty and luxury and peopled with the cream of French society, but she believes that it *can* be. Because she misconstrues life's limits so drastically, Emma soon finds herself hopelessly in debt, pressured by creditors and spurned by the lovers she accepted so eagerly.

Gustave Flaubert's *Madame Bovary* is the story of Emma's marriage, from the first colorful village feast to the end, when she plunges her hand into the rat poison and hungrily devours it, desperate to release herself from a world that has proven itself drab and below her romantic expectations.

After eating the fatal dose of poison, Emma ardently accepts the last rites. The priest dips his fingers into the oil and begins the annointments: first the eyes, "which had so fiercely coveted all earthly luxury;" then her lips, which cried out in lust; her hands, which had so longed for sensuous pleasure; and last, "the soles of her feet, once so swift in hurrying to gratify her desires, and now never to walk again."

Normandy is renowned for its fine veal, butter, cream and cheese. It is from the cooking of Normandy that French food gets its reputation for rich cream sauces. The area also produces a very fine apple, which is made into an alcoholic cider and the excellent liquor, Calvados. Emma's wedding feast reflects these Normandy specialties.

VEAL CASSEROLE

Preheat oven to 375 degrees F.

3	tablespoons butter
4	tablespoons flour
2	cups hot chicken stock
¾	cup sautéed onions
1	cup sautéed mushrooms
1/3	cup cream
½	cup grated Swiss cheese
	salt, pepper, and lemon juice to taste
6	slices cooked veal (leftover roast works well)
6	slices ham

Melt the butter in a heavy frying pan and blend in the flour to make a paste. Add the hot chicken stock and beat with a wire whisk until smooth and thickened. Stir in the cooked onions and mushrooms. Add the cream and simmer, stirring until the sauce is fairly thick. Add the seasoning and 2/3 of the cheese. Spread some of the sauce on the bottom of a baking dish. Lay the veal slices in the dish and cover them with ham slices. Add the rest of the sauce and sprinkle with the leftover cheese. Place the casserole in the oven and bake until it is lightly browned and bubbling.

CHICKEN FRICASSEE

1	chicken cut into serving size pieces
1	tablespoon butter
1	cup white wine
4	cups boiling water
20	pearl onions, peeled
1	cup chopped parsley
1	bay leaf
¼	teaspoon thyme
¼	teaspoon salt

pinch of ground pepper

2	tablespoons flour mixed with
3	tablespoons water
3	egg yolks

In a Dutch oven, or other heavy cooking pot, melt the butter, then add the chicken, browning on all sides. Add the wine, cover, and cook over medium-high heat until most of the wine has evaporated. Add the water, onions, parsley, bay leaf, thyme, salt, and pepper. Boil for 6 to 8 minutes, then stir in the flour paste. Partially cover, and cook for 20 to 25 more minutes on low heat. Add the mushrooms and cook another 20 minutes or so. Beat the egg yolks with a bit of the sauce, add to the chicken, and stir until slightly thickened. Serve with noodles, rice, or potatoes.

SORRELL CHIFFONNADE

Sorrel is a lemony flavored herb, often served as a garnish with meat, soup, or eggs. Emma Bovary serves it with veal.

Cut at least one bunch of sorrel into julienne strips. Cook it slowly in butter until it disintegrates, and serve.

MARASCHINO ICE

Maraschino is a liqueur made from the marasca cherry, native to Eastern Europe.

½   cup maraschino liqueur

1   quart cold sugar syrup

1   tablespoon fresh lemon juice

Freeze in an ice cream maker, following the manufacturer's directions for ices.

KIRSCH TODDY, THE BRIDE'S FATHER

Kirsch actually makes an acceptable toddy in a pinch.

1   teaspoon sugar syrup

1   stick cinnamon

1   jigger kirsch

1   cup very hot water

½   lemon slice

3   whole cloves

Put the sugar syrup, cinnamon stick, and kirsch in an 8 ounce mug. Add water. Stud the lemon slice with the cloves and decorate the edge of the mug with it.
Yield: 1 toddy

THE MEMBER OF THE WEDDING

by
Carson McCullers

The long hot days of August, once a part of the annual rhythm of life, are now largely a luxury enjoyed by only an indolent few. Air conditioning, frenetic work schedules, and summer school have relegated these precious oppressive afternoons to memory. Once people spent whole afternoons in idle conversation in summer's last assault, and like gardens in their final burst of growth before harvest, they allowed themselves to linger before the activity of autumn. Like the fruit on the vine, people ripen in late summer and become ready for the transformations that time of year can bring.

In Carson McCullers's enduring novella *The Member of the Wedding*, set in these dog days of August, twelve-year-old Frankie Adams is poised at the threshold of adolescence, struggling to let go of the familiar world of her childhood. For Frankie, this change is not gradual, but happens like a tectonic shift, over a single weekend. A tomboy in a pink organdy dress, she drags her juvenility grotesquely behind her, like a second skin that has been shed but not yet dropped completely away. One moment she plays with her six-year-old cousin, the next she changes her name to F. Jasmine Adams and sprinkles herself with Sweet Serenade toilet water.

So desperate is Frankie to escape the life she has led thus far that she fantasizes that her soldier brother and his fiancée, who are to be married in a few days in the nearby town of Winter Hill, will take her with them after the wedding to the wonderful world of anyplace else. She dreams of Maine, of Hollywood, of Eskimos, and of the war in Europe. When her brother was first sent to Alaska with the Armed Forces, she sent him home-made fudge and divinity. "It thrilled her to think that her fudge would be eaten in Alaska," and she imagined him passing it out to the Eskimos. To Frankie, Alaska is an exotic land of ice and snow caves, as different from her hometown as anywhere could be. So dedicated is Frankie to the idea of a wondrous world outside this small town that when she hears that her brother has been swimming in Alaska, she dismisses it from her mind, preferring to think of it romantically as the land of wintry magic.

Frankie lives with her widowed father, who spends long hours at his jewelry store. Her main companions are the family cook, Berenice, and the imp-like John Henry, her six-year-old cousin. The focal point of the novel is the family kitchen, where Frankie, Berenice, and John Henry converse desultorily, and where we watch Frankie's childhood drop away in a parade of grotesque images representing the distortion of a childhood clung to far too long: Frankie threatening the others with the butcher knife she uses to remove a splinter from her foot; the bespectacled John Henry hopping and skipping around the kitchen in imitation of the little pinhead in the carnival freak show; Frankie, looking, in Berenice's "candy opinion" like a human Christmas tree in an orange satin evening gown and dirty elbows. One moment touchingly vulnerable, the next, explosive and rebellious, Frankie emerges from her childhood over a meal of hopping john, baked sweet potatoes, cornbread, and buttermilk.

The three kitchenmates feast, alternately eating and talking, stretching out the afternoon until twilight. Frankie tells them that when she is in her coffin they should hold a plate of hopping john under her nose to make certain she's really dead, for if anything will bring her out of the deepest sleep, it's a plateful of black-eyed peas and rice. By turn, they each select their death tests: Berenice chooses a piece of fried fresh-water trout; and John Henry picks divinity fudge.

As the afternoon wears on, the three talk of love. Frankie has never spoken of love before, but listens raptly as Berenice enumerates the peculiar couplings she has seen: women in love with cloven-footed Satans; boys who fall in love with other boys; and her own third husband, who had "eatin dreams" and once swallowed a corner of the bed sheet. They suspend their conversation to pick delicately at the knuckle bone or to break open a sweet potato, concentrate on their eating a while, then pause for more conversation. "…they would eat awhile and let the food have a chance to spread out and settle inside their stomachs, and a little later they would start again."

A piano tuner begins his work in a nearby house, banging notes "in a solemn and crazy way," tormenting all the listeners. Against the dissonant music, Frankie models the dress she has bought for the wedding—an evening gown much too big for her. Storming around the room with her dirty elbows, orange satin, and her toes squeezed into silver slippers, Frankie laughs hysterically and pounds her fists as she struggles to be grown-up enough to wear the dress. And then they begin to eat again. Frankie takes off the dress and finishes the cold peas in her petticoat. And so on until twilight, eating, talking, eating…talking…"criticizing the work of the creator"…wondering what "hopping john" is called in France…as Frankie sheds her old skin in preparation for the next stage of life.

In the final chapter, Frankie's transformation from child to adolescent is complete. She and her father move into another house, and left are the old kitchen with its "crazy" walls full of children's drawings, along with Frankie's childhood and echoes of their voices over dinner.

000

HOPPING JOHN

Hopping john is good ol' black-eyed peas and rice, sometimes called, according to Berenice, "peas and rice," or "rice and peas and pot liquor." It is traditionally served on New Year's Day for good luck.

1	cup black-eyed peas
1	ham knuckle or hock
1	green pepper, seeded and chopped
1	onion, chopped
	water
1	tablespoon butter
1	pinch cayenne pepper
1	cup steamed rice
	salt and pepper to taste

Put the peas in a kettle and add water to cover. Bring to a boil; boil about two minutes, then cover, turn off the heat, and let stand for an hour. Add the knuckle or ham hock, green pepper, onion, and more water to cover. Simmer for about 2 hours. Add the rice, butter and cayenne, salt and pepper. Heat and stir until the butter melts.
Yield: 8 servings

DIVINITY FUDGE

1 ½	cups white or light brown sugar
½	cup water
1	teaspoon vinegar
1	egg white

½   teaspoon vanilla

½   cup chopped walnuts (optional)

Put in a saucepan the sugar, water, and vinegar. Cook over low heat to the
firm ball stage, (when a bit of the syrup dropped into cold water forms a ball
firm to the touch, or when the mixture reaches 244 degrees.) Beat the egg
white until stiff. Pour the sugar syrup slowly over the egg white, beating with
an electric mixer until creamy. Add the vanilla, and the walnuts, if desired.
Drop by teaspoonfuls on wax paper or spread in a buttered pan about 8x8
inches. Cut into squares and serve.
Yield: 16 squares

MOBY DICK AND "BARTELBY THE SCRIVENER"

by
Herman Melville

Herman Melville's gigantic novel, *Moby Dick*, a raging, roaring, storm-tossed hunt for a white whale which encompasses the conflicts between evil and innocence, faith and doubt, and the ultimate fallibility of humankind, begins as a simple hunt for a room and a meal on a frosty December night. On a "bitterly cheerless" dark and dismal night, Ishmael, a bored school teacher intent on adventure, roams the bowels of New Bedford, Massachusetts. He rejects The Crossed Harpoons and Sword-Fish Inn as too expensive and jolly and finally settles on The Spouter Inn owned, ominously, by a Mr. Peter Coffin. A likely looking place, Ishmael thinks, for a cheap bed and a cup of "pea coffee."

The palsied house sits on a sharp corner, a wintry wind howling through its unchinked crannies. In the entryway hangs a portentious representation of a ship, a whale, and a hurricane, battling one another for supremacy on the high seas. "A boggy, soggy, squitchy picture, truly enough to drive a nervous man distracted." Across the dark low-ceilinged lobby is the bar, fashioned inside the giant jaw-bone of a whale, where the barkeep Jonah "sells the sailors deliriums and death." He serves his poison in deceitful glasses with tapered bottoms—known as "cheaters" to the initiated. Carved into the side of each glass is a measure. This much for a penny, this much for two pennies, "and so on to the full glass—the Cape Horn measure, which you may gulp down for a schilling," presumably a straight shot to cure the loneliness of years at sea. He also vends a mixture of gin and molasses to cure catarrh.

103

Old seadogs hunch in the dim and dusty corners—examining, whittling, examining again—the sailor's endless pastime. The house is full, not a bed to let, but Ishmael is welcome to share with a mysterious harpooner by the exotic name of Quequeeg, out at the moment—"peddling heads."

"Supper'll be ready directly."

The dining room is as cold as Iceland, but the fire is welcome. By the oily light of two tallow candles, with monkey jackets buttoned to the neck and icy fingers clutching cutlery, the sailors at The Spouter Inn tuck into meat and potatoes and dumplings at tea.

Ishmael thinks highly of cooks. There is a glory of a sort in going to sea as a cook. "...a cook being a sort of officer on ship-board...once broiled, judiciously buttered, and judgmatically salted and peppered, there is no one who will speak more respectfully, not to say reverentially, of a boiled fowl than I will." It is no wonder then that the author devotes two full chapters "Breakfast" and "Chowder" to Ishmael's gustatory descriptions.

"Grub, ho!" cries Peter Coffin, enthusiastically announcing the morning meal. But the old seadogs approach the dining room self-consciously. Although they may have dueled with great whales on the high seas, rubbed shoulders with the exotic in distant ports, and drunk the "Cape Horn measure" with a fervor to rival Father Mapple's sermon, they are shy and embarrassed at the table.

Solemnly, they enter the breakfast room, and whether from social discomfort or the effects of last night's deliriums, they dabble in coffee and rolls while Ishmael's new roommate, Quequeeg, self-assuredly spears rare beefsteaks with his ever-present harpoon. Oddly, the same men the night before showed no signs of ill ease with their dumplings. Fortified with demon rum, dumplings may have been tasty fare indeed, but even Ishmael seems somewhat disinterested in the morning repast.

Later, on Nantucket, however, Ishmael becomes rapturous over the New England whaling village staple; chowder. Ishmael and Quequeeg have traveled by schooner from New Bedford to the town from which they hope to set sail. It is once again late evening and the pair set out to find room and repast. On recommendation of Peter Coffin, they head for "Try Pots," owned by Coffin's cousin, famous for its chowders.

"Clam or cod?" asks the hostess, Mrs. Hussey. The fragrant kitchen steam whets their famished appetites and sends Ishmael into poetic flights: "Oh, sweet friends! hearken to me!" Clams no bigger than hazelnuts, pounded ship's biscuits, flakes of smoky salt pork, butter and seasonings! A second bowl-full, this time of cod, sends the sailors off to their rooms, satisfied and contented.

000

MOBY DICK CLAM CHOWDER

The following recipe is a version of the traditional chowder that has been served in New England for generations.

1	quart clams in the shell
1	cup water
4	slices salt pork, minced
1	small onion, thinly sliced
4	medium potatoes, peeled and boiled
3	cups scalded milk
1	tablespoon flour
1	tablespoon butter
	freshly ground pepper
	soda crackers

Scrub the clams and put them in a large pot with the water. Cover, bring to a boil and cook until the clams open. Remove the clams from the shells, chop the meat and return to the pot. In a frying pan, fry the salt pork until crisp. Remove the salt pork from the pan and sauté the onions until soft. Combine the clams, the onions, potatoes (diced and slightly mashed,), clam liquor and pepper. Cook 10 minutes. Add the scalded milk and bring to a boil. Finally, add the flour and butter, kneaded together. Bring to a boil again, and serve with the crackers to add as desired.

Yield: 4-6 servings

*The great whaling story is not alone in revealing a Melville character's appreciation of his victuals. In **Bartleby the Scrivener**, his memorable tale of passive resistance, the author describes his characters in terms of what they eat. The self-indulgent Turkey wears clothes that smell of food; Nippers suffers from fits of indigestion; and Ginger Nut, whose duties include the fetching of cakes and apples for his workmates, is named for the cakes he purveys. "…small, flat, round, and very spicy…" they are vended cheaply near the office, and Turkey and Nippers gobble them up by the score.*

Bartleby lives on nothing but these spicy confections which, by their description, are what we today call "gingersnaps," that staple of the nursery kitchen.

BARTELBY'S GINGER NUTS

1	cup light molasses
1	cup sugar
¾	cup butter
4 ½	cups sifted all-purpose flour
1/3	cup water
1	teaspoon baking soda
1	tablespoon ground ginger
1	teaspoon ground nutmeg

Preheat oven to 375 degrees F.

Combine molasses, sugar, and butter in a saucepan and bring just to a boil. Cool slightly. Sift together the flour, soda and spices. Add dry ingredients to the liquid mixture, along with the water, and blend well. Chill this dough thoroughly, then roll out on a floured surface. Cut with a floured cookie cutter and place on a greased baking sheet. Bake at 375 degrees about 8 minutes. Transfer the cookies to a rack for cooling. Yield: about 56 cookies.

NOTE: take care that they don't burn, because a burned ginger nut is a bitter nut, indeed!

A MOVEABLE FEAST

by
Ernest Hemingway

When the greatest literary legend of the twentieth century, Ernest Heming-way, returned to the Ritz Hotel in Paris in 1956, where he had spent the liberation in World War II, one of the porters still working there mentioned two trunks of Hemingway's that had been sitting in the basement storage for years, awaiting the return of the hotel's most famous resident. Upon opening the forgotten trunks, Hemingway found them filled with memorabilia from the time he spent in Paris in the 1920s with his first wife, Hadley.

From the contents of the trunks he began to reconstruct those early, heady days in a book that was to add another layer to the patina of Paris between the wars, *A Moveable Feast*. The book is a memoir of a middle-aged man looking back 30 years through a filter of time that is bound to result in reinterpretation of incidents and of people. In fact, Hemingway tells us in his preface to the book that readers are free to regard it as fiction, but that "...there is always a chance that such a book of fiction may throw some light on what has been written as fact."

The 25-year-old Earnest Hemingway and his young wife Hadley had a small, but steady income in those years. She had an annual stipend from an inheritance, and he was a newspaper correspondent, regularly selling stories to the American and Canadian press, but they kept themselves on a severe budget in order to finance his interests in sports and travel. By shaving as much as possible off the rent, they were able to afford many of the pleasures Europe offered cheaply in the early twenties. Thus Hemingway, Hadley, and their baby lived in a shabby two-room flat on Rue Cardinal Lemoine, in an unsavory part of Paris. The flat had a fireplace in the bedroom and a big bed, although the bathroom was a small closet with only a pitcher, a bowl, and a slop jar, and the kitchen was also tiny. Despite their frugality, the couple had a wonderful Breton cook, Marie Cocotte, who introduced them to the cuisine of France. In the memoir, Hemingway particularly remembers one of Marie's lunches, which he devoured hungrily after spending the morning at Sylvia Beach's book shop: *foie de veau* with mashed potatoes, accompanied by an endive salad and little radishes, and an apple tart for dessert. "We ate well and cheaply and drank well and cheaply and slept well and warm together and loved each other," the now-mature writer says of the young writer and his wife.

Hemingway was in his mid-twenties at the time—athletic, with a large appetite. But sometimes, he says, he skipped meals in order to have enough money to travel and to follow the ponies. At these times he would tell Hadley that he'd been invited to lunch, but would instead walk for two hours in the Luxembourg Gardens, where there was no smell of good things to eat to taunt his hunger.

But his was a hunger that sharpened the senses, and Hemingway would go to see the Cézannes at the Luxembourg museum instead of eating. Cézanne's paintings became a major influence on the new writing style Hemingway was developing, one that emphasized physical objects, action, accurate rendering of dialogue, and minimal description.

After leaving the museum, Hemingway would choose a route that passed no restaurants or tempting food shops, walk to the Place St. Sulpice, and then away from the river to the Rue de l'Odeon to Sylvia Beach's bookshop, Shakespeare and Company, to pick up his mail. On one particular day there was money from the sale of a story, and the young writer headed for Lipp's and ordered a very large glass of cold, foamy beer and potato salad. The *pommes l'huille* were firm and drenched in olive oil. He ground black pepper over them, dipped his crusty bread in the oil, and ate slowly and appreciatively, then ordered *cervelas*, the same sausage known in England as 'saveloy' enjoyed by David Copperfield when he had the money.

Paris was filled with many young writers in circumstances similar to Hemingway's, and they all found a warm welcome at Sylvia Beach's bookstore. It had a big stove with a fire in winter, shelves and shelves of books, a rental library, the latest gossip, and the friendship of its owner, who mothered them, sometimes published them, as in the case of James Joyce's *Ulysses* and even sometimes lent them money.

In those days, recalls Hemingway, two people could live well on five dollars a day and still travel. The Hemingways traveled to Spain, Switzerland, and Germany for fishing and skiing. They stayed in cozy lodges, snuggled in bed together with the windows open, smelling the cold, clean mountain air. They ate *trout au bleu*, washing it down with Sion wine and the view of the Dent du Medi, and after skiing, jugged hare with red wine (more expensive than the white at 20 cents a liter). And always they had piles of wonderful books, lent to them by Sylvia Beach.

Like Scott and Zelda Fitzgerald, Ernest Hemingway and Hadley Hemingway have attained the status of myth. Their own lives have become stories in which they are the characters, and what many readers want is not so much to read Hemingway, but to *be* Hemingway, to be bigger than life, to eat more, drink more, love more, to live more than ordinary mortals.

A Moveable Feast was written in Hemingway's last years. The visit to the Ritz when he discovered the trunks was the beginning of a period of extreme self-doubt that culminated in serious depression. He felt that as a writer, he was at the end of his powers after winning the Nobel Prize in 1954. He had survived injuries in two plane crashes, believed that the FBI was following him, and after undergoing shock treatments, voluntarily left the Mayo Clinic, desperate to kill himself. Paranoid, delusional, obsessed with thoughts of suicide, he attempted to recreate the past in his last book, and a creation it is, in places. He has been particularly criticized for his treatments of Gertrude Stein, Ford Maddox Ford and F. Scott Fitzgerald. He ignores his unhappiness at Hadley's pregnancy and omits other significant details which, if included, might have given a less romantic look at literary Paris in the 1920s, and perhaps a more complex view of some of the characters which surrounded the young writer and his wife.

In an early chapter, Hemingway remembers walking home from the racetrack with Hadley, both of them full of themselves, of life, of Paris, and of nostalgia for a fishing trip they had once taken with their old friend Chink.

They stopped at Michaud's, where James Joyce regularly ate with his family. Waiting for a table, perhaps fearful of seeming sentimental, even to himself, Hemingway asks Hadley how much of their previous mood could have been just the effects of ordinary hunger. She answered that there are many kinds of hunger. Memory, she says, is a kind of hunger.

000

FOIE de VEAU

Calves' liver, not a popular entrée in the United States, is positively elegant when cooked in the French manner.

1	pound calves' liver
¼	cup flour
2	tablespoons butter
½	cup white wine
1	teaspoon lemon juice
1	tablespoon chopped parsley

Coat the liver slices with the flour and sauté in 1 tablespoon of the butter until the liver is done to your liking. You may wish to cook it quickly at high heat for rare, or more slowly at medium heat for medium or well-done. Remove the cooked liver from the pan and keep it warm. Add the wine to the pan and whisk it until smooth and slightly thickened. Stir in the remaining tablespoon of butter, the lemon juice, and the parsley. Pour the sauce over the liver slices and serve.

Yield: 4 servings

ENDIVE SALAD

Not to be confused with the salad green sometimes known as curly endive, Belgian endive is a pale ivory-colored vegetable that has a somewhat spike-like shape with a pleasant, bitter taste, and a high price.

Wash your endives carefully, slice them crosswise into small pieces, and dress with vinaigrette.

APPLE TART

The French apple tart, believe it or not, is lower in fat than most, as it does not have a cream filling.

Your recipe for single pie crust dough

2	medium apples
2	cups sweetened applesauce
½	cup apricot jam
1	tablespoon water

Preheat oven to 375 degrees.

Line a tart pan or pie plate with the dough. Fill with the applesauce, spreading it evenly in the dish. Peel, core and slice the apples and lay them over the applesauce. You can arrange them in an attractive pattern if you wish. Bake about 40 minutes. Remove from the oven and let cool a bit while you heat the apricot jam and water together in a small saucepan, stirring until smooth. Spread the thinned jam over the top of the tart.

POMMES DE TERRE a L'HUILE

Small red potatoes work well for French potato salad.

2	lbs. boiling potatoes
2	tablespoons dry, white vermouth
2	tablespoons chicken stock
½	cup vinaigrette
2	tablespoons chopped scallions or other mild onion
2	tablespoons chopped parsley

Boil the potatoes until tender. Peel and slice, then toss them with the vermouth and broth and let them stand until the liquid has been absorbed by the potatoes. Finally, toss with the remaining ingredients. Serve at room temperature.
Yield: 8 servings

MY ANTONIA

by
Willa Cather

A wholesome childhood, the smell of baking from the kitchen oven, and Grandma in her apron are perhaps at the center of the American mythology. Add loyal friendship and a willingness to help the less fortunate and you will have our traditional view of how life should be. The simple rural lifestyles have always been our ideal: generous-hearted farmers and loyal hired hands providing a secure nest for the young, while at the same time offering assistance to neighbors in need. This ideal is the subject of Willa Cather's *My Antonia*, a portrait of the citizens of a rural mid-western community of nearly a century ago. The smells of Grandmother Burden's kitchen surround us as we, through the narration of her grandson Jim, meet the Shimerdas, newly-arrived immigrants from Eastern Europe. The newcomers endure the hardship of a prairie winter in a dug-out cave, sustaining themselves on a diet of corncakes and molasses until they are "adopted" by their kindly neighbors.

Grandmother Burden, with her homespun ways, is a disciplined, hard working American farm woman, at once critical of the "foreign" habits of her new neighbors and compassionate and protective of their inborn dignity as human beings. The handmade quilts, wood stove, and white-washed floors of her home contrast with the grime and fetid odor of kerosene and rotted potatoes in the Shimerda's cave. Unlike the Burdens, these immigrants are hot-tempered, mean-spirited, and despondent. As Hermione Lee points out in her critical biography of Cather, *Double Lives*, housekeeping in Cather's novels is reflective of the moral qualities of the characters. Each stitch, scrub, and stir represents respect for God's world. A home as slovenly as the Shimerda cave bespeaks a lack of respect for one's existence. Hard work and attention to the physical needs of the family are the outward signs of the value of human life.

At the helm of the flour bin for most of the paean to a lost way of life, Jim's grandmother polishes, scrubs, kneads and stitches like our own prototypical grandma, hands smelling of the sink hug strong and enveloping.

Even though Jim's grandmother is offended by the ways of her new neighbors, her subsequent "adoption" of Antonia, the oldest Shimerda daughter, is a testament to her own moral housekeeping. Schooled in housewifery by Grandmother Burden, Antonia becomes, at the end of the story, an icon for the moral spirit of the Midwest. Once a humble and unkempt immigrant from a family unknowledgeable about making a living from the land, Antonia matures into an industrious, upright American farm woman.

The story is told in flashback as Jim, a successful writer and man of the world, returns to his old home to visit Antonia and her family. Now fully representative of the rural idea of the harmonious rhythms of planting, tending, and harvesting, his childhood friend has redeemed her squalid beginnings. Jars of home-canned cherries and strawberries glint in the sunlight, and fruitful orchards display their rewards for the sweat and tears invested in them.

Antonia is immensely proud of her hard work. Like Jay Gatsby tossing his silk shirts on the bed for Daisy's admiration, Antonia takes Jim on a tour of her cupboards. Whole pickles, chopped pickles, watermelon rind and crabapples twinkle in glass jars, surrounded by the smell of rising bread dough and the sounds of a dozen children.

"Next to getting warm and keeping warm, dinner and supper were the most interesting things we had to think about," says Jim Burden in reference to his growing-up years on the great middle-American prairie. "On Sundays she gave us as much chicken as we could eat," he reminisces, "and on other days we had ham or bacon and sausage meat. She baked either pies or cakes for us every day, unless, for a change she made my favorite pudding, striped with currants and boiled in a bag."

It was heavy fare, but typical of the hard-working, calorie burning farmers of the Midwest at the turn of the century. Working from sun-up until sundown, seven days a week, and isolated in the long cold winters, they depended upon food for entertainment, as well as nourishment. The rhythm of the seemingly incessant baking of Jim's childhood is broken only by the Saturday night corn-popping or taffy-pulling, and the strains of the hired man's harmonica, lonesomely rendering "For I am a young cowboy and I know I've done wrong."

000

JIM BURDEN'S FAVORITE TAFFY WITH WALNUTS

Now largely relegated to Girl Scout meetings, the taffy pull is a lost part of Americana well worth reviving, if not for the sociability it creates, at least for its toothsome results. In its hey-day, taffy was such a popular confection that kitchens without enough hands for pulling often had a metal hook attached to a wall so that one person could do the job, using the hook as an extra pair of hands.

For best results, have all participants wash and butter their hands after the taffy begins to cool, just as it becomes ripe for pulling. Each pair of pullers takes a fist-sized glob of the taffy and pulls it out into a long strand before doubling it back and pulling it out again. Do this over and over, until the taffy refuses to stick to itself. When the taffy has become completely hardened, it can be cracked into small pieces and stored.

1	cup sugar
1/8	teaspoon cream of tartar
2	tablespoons butter
½	cup vinegar
¼	cup chopped walnuts

Line a buttered dinner plate or small platter with the nuts. Mix all other ingredients in a saucepan and boil on high heat, stirring constantly, to a hard ball stage. Then immediately pour onto the plate. When cool enough to handle, start pulling with buttered hands. Do not let the taffy get hard before pulling!

CURRANT BOILED PUDDING

Admittedly this old fashioned boiled pudding does not have the most appetizing appearance by modern standards, but it tastes just as earthy and wholesome as a Boston brown bread. Puddings of Jim Burden's time were actually boiled in a bag, often a homemade one, although at that time it was possible to buy a manufactured one. Nowadays, however, they are next to impossible to find, so you'll probably have to make your own.

Pudding bag:

Fold a large, clean, closely-woven cotton dish towel or diaper into four thick-nesses and sew up two sides to make a bag. The bag must be covered with flour paste to prevent leakage of the batter through the porous fabric. To do this, first soak the bag in hot water and wring it out, then sprinkle both sides generously with flour, and "slop" it around until the coating is the consistency of a paste and covers the bag completely. Now turn the bag inside out and repeat the process. Turn the bag so that the smooth seam is inside.

Mix thoroughly the following ingredients:

1	cup molasses
1	cup water
1	teaspoon baking soda
2	cups whole wheat pastry flour
1	cup dried currants

Pour this mixture into the pudding bag. In order to leave enough room for expansion, fill the bag no more than half full. Close it tightly at the end with a wire twist. There should be room in the bag for the pudding to expand. Sub-merge it completely in boiling water. Be sure to keep the water boiling throughout the cooking of the pudding, which should be about three hours. Remove the bag from the water, dip it in cold water, and slip the pudding out onto a plate. When first out of the bag, it looks awful—but be patient; it gets better looking as it cools. When cool, the pudding texture will be slightly gummy. Slice and serve.
Yield: 12 servings

THE RAZOR'S EDGE

by
Somerset Maugham

Somerset Maugham's popular period piece, *The Razor's Edge*, set between the devastations of World War I and the stock market crash of 1929, is unusual in the Maugham canon in that nearly all of its characters are Americans. While some of the action does take place in Chicago, the tale is played out mostly in Europe. The characters are well-to-do and can afford the trappings of their class: genuine antiques, pitchers of martinis, and newly-deposed European royalty, now beholden to others for invitations and a possible free meal. Paris, in this novel, seems filled both with now somewhat tarnished aristocracy and those who covet the patina such associations might give to their social reputations.

Leading the chase of the pretenders is Elliott Templeton, expatriate American and social climber extroardinaire. As Maugham tells us in the first pages of the novel, Elliott is always elegantly turned out, his haberdashery from Charvet's and the rest—shoes, suits, and hats—came from the best shops in London. He has an exquisite apartment in a fashionable section of Paris, knows all the right people, and to his credit has no visible means of support. Those who wished to be unkind said that he dealt in antique furniture and art, and that after he had entertained wealthy Americans at a fine luncheon, one or two drawings or a small table would vanish, but on the whole, Elliot could not be accused of having ungentlemanly concerns. Although he will go to any lengths to meet the "right people" and has a weakness for the old and great names, his saving grace is that he knows this about himself, and accepts it as any other human weakness. As Maugham states, "Elliot was too clever not to see that many of the persons who accepted his invitations did so only to get a free meal, and that of these, some were unworthy of his time, but he simply cannot resist the glamour of a title. He has a natural romanticism, and the ability to see that in the distant lineage of any 'weedy little French duke' is a crusader in the Holy Land."

Elliot has been living in Europe for a very long time and has all but lost the American predilection for hard work, plain speaking, and wholesome living, exhibited by his sister and niece: the Bradleys of Chicago. Twenty-year-old Isabel Bradley is in love with Larry Darrell, a taciturn young man, who unlike either the Paris or Chicago branches of Isabel's family, lives life without ulterior motives of any kind. He, too, becomes an American expatriate in Paris, but unlike Uncle Elliot, stretches his very modest allowance to afford a shabby room and a life of serious study among the artists, writers, and students of the Latin Quarter. Larry reads only for the pleasure of reading and invites people to lunch solely to enjoy their company.

Before his Paris sojourn, Larry refused a job with a Chicago brokerage firm, a job that would have brought with it the kind of life Isabel and her mother feel is not only financially desirable, but the morally right thing to do for their country, which is developing at a rapid, invigorating pace and needs all its sons to help. In refusing the job, Larry makes a match between himself and Isabel impossible. "A man ought to work. That's what he's here for. That's how he contributes to the welfare of his community."

While they are still in Chicago, in an effort to get Larry alone to convince him of the rightness of hard work, Isabel arranges a day in the country for them. Uncle Elliot, visiting Chicago from Paris, insists that they take a picnic hamper of paté de foie gras, curried shrimps, breast of chicken in aspic, hearts-of-lettuce salad, a bottle of Montrachet, and—a concession to their American habits—an apple pie. But imposing their simple American tastes, Mrs. Bradley sends along stuffed eggs, chicken sandwiches, and a thermos of coffee (though Isabel tucks in a pitcher of martinis as a precaution against the stress of such a life-defining conversation). Typically, Elliott blames the failure of the above meeting on the menu, for to him style is substance, and style has the power to change events and feelings. To his American relatives, however, style is merely an added decoration.

Though Larry Darrell rejects the materialism of both Europe and the United States, Maugham draws a distinction between the two. While Europe, particularly France, values appearances, American money symbolizes the health and vigor of a young country, striving to find its place at the top.

The false and haggard face of Europe is evident in Elliott's two American protégés, women who came to France when they were young and put themselves under Elliott's tutelage to be "done over" for their launching into Paris society. They dress in the best couture, but are heavily made-up, have dyed hair, and "hungry restless eyes" that betray their struggle to cling to their first youth. Their conversation is inane, and their voices unnaturally bright and agitated, and to Isabel they seem "...afraid if they were silent for an instant the machine would run down and the artificial construction which was all they were would fall to pieces."

Maugham contrasts them to the vibrant Isabel: "Isabel, with her youth, her strapping good looks, and her vitality, brought a breath of fresh air into that meretricious atmosphere. She swept in like a young earth goddess. The two American ladies, with shrill amiabilities on their lips, looked her up and down, took in the details of her dress, and perhaps in their hearts felt a pang of dismay at being confronted with her exuberant youth."

The difference between the women is the difference between the overly rich and decadent picnic Elliott prescribes and the simpler American lunch the Bradley's prefer.

000

Aspics, now out of fashion, were a mainstay on the luncheon tables between the two world wars. Unlike the cloying Jello and cottage cheese concoctions popular at post World War II Tupperware parties, aspics were often substantial main course dishes.

Chicken aspic can be made and served in your best glass bowl, or you can use a mold. If you decide to use a mold, dip the bottom in warm water and turn the aspic out onto a bed of greens just before serving.

CHICKEN BREAST IN ASPIC

2	cups boiling chicken stock
1	tablespoon unflavored gelatin
¼	cup cold water
2-3	cups diced chicken breast

For decoration, add 1 to 2 cups of any combination of the following:

Sliced hard boiled eggs

sliced pimento

stuffed olives

cooked sliced carrots

cooked broccoli flowerets

canned mushrooms

Soak the gelatin in the water. Add it to the boiling stock and stir until dissolved. Chill until it begins to set, then layer the gelatin mixture with the chicken and whichever ingredients you've chosen to use in the bowl or mold. Chill until firm. Serve with curried mayonnaise, below.
Yield: 6 servings

Chilled prawns dipped in curried mayonnaise make a simple but elegant picnic starter. Plan 1/4 pound of cooked, peeled and chilled prawns per person. The curried mayonnaise can accompany both the aspic and the prawns.

CURRIED MAYONNAISE

1	cup mayonnaise
¼	teaspoon ground ginger
1	teaspoon curry powder
1	teaspoon honey
1	tablespoon lemon juice

Thoroughly combine all ingredients and serve.

TRADITIONAL MARTINI

By the 1950s, any self-respecting, pencil-moustached rake would no more have been without his cocktail pitcher and stash of olives than he would without his mono-grammed smoking jacket. The following martini is typical of Isabel's day, when a 3 martini lunch didn't mean a hangover by dinner time.

The original martini, half gin and half vermouth, was a very weak sister, indeed, to the extra dry 60-to-1 version of the drink that became popular in the 1970s. This knock-out punch called for 3 ounces of gin with just a splash of vermouth to top it off.

For each drink:

1 ½	ounces dry gin
¾	ounce dry vermouth
1	pitted green olive

Fill a cocktail pitcher with cracked ice. Pour the gin slowly over the ice, and then pour in the vermouth. Stir briskly, and strain into glasses (or a thermos if you are taking it on the road). Add an olive to each drink before serving.

REBECCA

by
Daphne du Maurier

In Daphne du Maurier's suspenseful masterpiece, *Rebecca*, the unnamed narrator, second wife of the aristocratic Maxim de Winter, creeps into the world of her glamorous predecessor, stumbling clumsily through her home and social life, and into the cunning traps laid by Mrs. Danvers, the sinister housekeeper, loyal to her lady even after death. The young Mrs. de Winter's self consciousness as mistress of Manderley, one of the most elegant manor houses in England, is pathetic—almost comic. Fearful of the servants, she sneaks biscuits and fruit from her own dining room, secretes the pieces of a broken ornament, hides from her guests in the servants' quarters.

The youthful and inexperienced outsider interprets the tense expressions and noncommittal remarks Rebecca's name elicits as grief at her death, and disappointment in her plain, shy replacement. Not until very late in the novel do we find out that rather than having been loved and admired by those close to her, Rebecca engendered hatred and embarrassment because of her vulgar sensual appetites.

Young, orphaned, and lower-middle class, the new wife finds life at Manderley not only intimidating, but confusing and distastefully extravagant. She comes down on her first morning to a breakfast buffet of coffee, tea, scrambled eggs, bacon, fish, boiled eggs, porridge, ham, scones, toast, a selection of jams and marmalade, honey and piles of fruit—for two people. Although she is shocked at the waste of this daily spread, she never dares to ask if the leftovers are given to the poor, or simply shoveled into the garbage.

As she sits at her first Manderley tea, dreaming of the jubilant sounds of children and a future littered with cricket bats and toys, the butler sets out "tiny crisp wedges of toast, and piping-hot, flaky scones. Sandwiches of unknown nature, mysteriously flavoured and quite delectable, and that very special gingerbread. Angel cake, that melted in the mouth, and its rather stodgier companion bursting with peel and raisins."

Her first chore as mistress of Manderley is to approve the luncheon menu: curried prawns, roast veal, asparagus, cold chocolate mousse—but she cannot order the sauces and wines to accompany the food: "...whatever you think Mrs. de Winter would have ordered," she says, giving up her own home to the ghost of the dead Rebecca.

The narrator is the most passive of heroines, accepting the husband and the life left behind by another. In fact, when we are first introduced to her, before her marriage, she is sitting in a restaurant meekly receiving, from a disdainful waiter, a plate of ham and tongue, already sent back to the kitchen by another patron.

Most readers remember the innocent narrator in residence at Manderley taunted by the unhinged Mrs. Danvers and the memory of Rebecca, but the first chapters reveal what has happened to the de Winters after the destruction depicted on the last page of the novel. The couple abides in exile, the glaring Mediterranean sun exposing every corner and fleck of dust on the indifferent hotel balcony, in sharp contrast to the thick and twisted undergrowth of Manderley, its shadows and hidden trysting places.

Maxim de Winter, husband first to Rebecca and then to the innocent waif who tells us their tale, was goaded into the murder of his first wife. Forever scarred, he and his new wife are denied the pleasure of children, friends, and a routine country life. Instead, they must pay for this crime by dislocation and ennui.

In the end, Manderley is gone, and the de Winters have no new place for themselves. They wander about the continent, reading the news of the English country life which no longer belongs to them. They live out of suit-cases, and seem to own nothing. Although the stultifying regularity of their new life is a comfort to them both, they now, from afar, have steeped themselves in their former society as they never could have in the shadows cast by Manderley and the secrets of the past. They anxiously await the mail from England for news of dog racing in remote counties, the salmon run, and the price of cattle. Among the incandescent vineyards of their southern retreat, no children drag their toys into the library, no family dog fronts the fireplace, as the young wife imagined at that first tea at Manderley. There is only a bare, anonymous hotel table set for two, and nothing but bread and butter for tea.

000

As the narrator begins her tale of Manderley, she remembers the ritual of tea, and perhaps nothing so represents English country manor life.

SCONES

Scones, now popular in the United States (pronounced sconz by the English), are easy to make. They are basically sweet baking powder biscuits. For the best texture, the butter should be cold when you cut it in, and the dough handled as little as possible.

Preheat the oven to 450 degrees.

1 ¾	cups white flour
1	tablespoon sugar
2 ¼	teaspoons baking powder
½	teaspoon salt
¼	cup butter
2	eggs
½	cup cream

Sift the dry ingredients together. Cut in the butter, using a pastry blender. In a separate bowl, beat the eggs, and set aside two tablespoons. To the remaining beaten eggs, add the cream and mix well. Make a well in the center of the dry ingredients, add the liquid, and quickly stir all together. Place the dough on a lightly floured board, and pat it to about 3/4 inch thickness. Cut into squares or diamonds of desired size with a knife. Brush with the reserved egg, sprinkle with sugar, and bake for 15 minutes.
YIELD: 6 SCONES

CUCUMBER TEA SANDWICHES

Tea sandwiches should be made from white or soft wheat bread, trimmed of the crusts.

mayonaise

very thinly sliced cucumber

bread, trimmed of the crusts

Spread the bread with mayonnaise, cover with a layer of cucumber slices. Add the top pieces of bread and cut diagonally into quarters.

WATERCRESS TEA SANDWICHES

mayonaise

watercress, washed carefully

bread, trimmed of the crusts

Finely chop the watercress and mix with the mayonnaise to moisten. Spread the bread with this mixture. Add the top piece of bread and cut as with the cucumber tea sandwiches.

GINGERBREAD

Preheat the oven to 350 degrees

½   cup shortening

¼   cup brown sugar

1   egg

½   cup molasses

1 ½   cups sifted flour

½   teaspoon salt

¾   teaspoon baking soda

½   teaspoon ginger

½   teaspoon cinnamon

½   cup boiling water

Cream together the shortening and sugar. Add the egg and molasses and beat well. Sift together the dry ingredients and add to the creamed mixture alternately with the water, beating constantly until well blended. Put in a greased and floured small baking pan about 7 inches square and bake for 30 to 40 minutes or until the cake tests done.

SISTER CARRIE

by
Theodore Dreiser

Sister Carrie by Theodore Dreiser was one of the first "small town girl goes to the big city" stories. We've all read and seen the plot in old movies dozens of times since. A young, innocent woman arrives in the big town with only a little money in her pocket, hoping to find success in whatever form she conceives of it. Along the road to a good job, her first Broadway hit, or finding her prince charming, she undergoes a number of trials, some of which involve her virtue. In the end, she succeeds at whatever it is she's attempting, sometimes looking down from her lofty perch in the final chapter over the scattered remains of those who have helped her at their own sacrifice.

In this kind of novel—whether it be New York, Chicago, or Dickens' London—the city itself almost becomes one of the characters. Its teeming streets, its many pleasures and its dangers taunt and delight, threaten and reward. "Making it" there is a challenge, and the city dances with the characters according to its own particular tune. Just as Paris seduces and New York entraps, Chicago—that "toddlin' town"—can sweep you off your feet. Newly rebuilt after its infamous fire, Dreiser's Chicago is a vigorous city of "rotund, rosy...silk-hatted, starchy-bosomed, beringed and bescarf-pinned" nouveau riches looking for ways to make and spend a buck.

The new railroads have just made cross-country travel accessible, and small-town shoppers the country over are no longer limited to such merchandise as a local general store or the Sears and Roebuck catalogue can offer. Now many stores in each community can be filled with goods that come from anywhere between Philadelphia and California, and these goods are peddled by a new army of "drummers," or traveling salesmen, criss-crossing the country with a smile and a shoeshine. All this means jobs—factory work and sales work in the new "department stores."

In 1889, Carrie Meeber arrives in Chicago, poor, unsophisticated and impressionable. She is dazzled by the fashionable clothing, delicate lingerie, baubles of every kind, all displayed in the large sparkling plate-glass windows of these new emporia. There are stationery, footwear, dress goods, dainty skirts and petticoats, laces, and trinkets of all kinds attracting swarms of patrons, parading up and down the aisles, anxious to participate in this feeding frenzy of the new social Darwinism. Besides the fabulous stores brimming with goods are theaters showing little farces, buggies for hire, bright lights, and successful men with money enough to pay for it all.

But as Carrie finds out, the pleasures of Chicago are far above the meager fortunes of a girl on her own. Her dreams of fine petticoats and carriages soon dissolve, for the only work she can find is "on the line" in a sweat shop, punching eye holes in shoes. The work is tedious, the hours long, and the working conditions, typical of the time, are deplorable. The workers sit for hours on end in the hot, noisy room and can use the filthy bathrooms only during breaks. Carrie can afford nothing more than a bowl of soup at the sparkling lunch counters which so impress her, and at the end of the day must trudge home, even though her back is aching, because she can't pay for the trolley ride to the dreary flat she shares with her parsimonious sister and brother-in-law.

It is not long, however, before Carrie is rescued by her first beau, a nattily-dressed traveling salesman who is as superficial and impressionable as she is. For Carrie, Charles Drouet embodies all that is new and wonderful about the city. He is a flashy young swain who knows his way around town and likes pretty young women. He takes Carrie out to the Windsor dining room for her first restaurant meal ever and impresses her by ordering sirloin and mushrooms, stuffed tomatoes, hash brown potatoes, and asparagus. By the end of the meal he has convinced her to allow him to buy her some new clothes, and a short time later they are sharing a "swell" little flat, and Carrie is no longer obliged to work for her living.

Two years and several thousand dollars in stolen funds later, Carrie has struggled to a slightly higher position in the contest for survival of the fittest. She is now living, meretriciously, in New York, with a man who has better taste, but not with a lot more money than Drouet. Still, she is finally meeting the kind of people she aspires to be connected with—sophisticated, uncomplicated, and rich. One evening, while dining with some of them at Sherry's restaurant, a new rival of the great Delmonico's, Carrie assesses her progress by comparing this "temple of gastronomy" to the merely good restaurant where she dined with her first lover. She thinks back to when she wandered the Chicago streets, cold and hungry and at her wit's end, and observes the contrast between that first restaurant and this. She notes "the name of 'Tiffany' upon the silverware...'Haviland' upon the china..." the candleglow and the highly polished woodwork, and the waiters' air of attentiveness. "Each waiter added an air of exclusiveness and elegance by the manner in which he bowed, scraped, touched and trifled with things. The exclusively personal attention which he devoted to each one, standing half-bent, ear to one side, elbows akimbo, saying "soup—green turtle, yes—One portion—yes. Oysters—certainly—half-dozen—yes. Asparagus! Olives—yes." Or as the author puts it, "that exhibition of showy, wasteful and unwholesome gastronomy as practiced by wealthy Americans which is the wonder and astonishment of true culture and dignity the world over."

In the last chapter of the novel, Carrie, now the toast of Broadway, stands musing at the window of her suite at the Waldorf. Glancing down at the endless procession of humanity in the wintry night, she yawns.

000

TURTLE SOUP

Turtle soup is a traditional English speciality, served at ceremonial dinners. Its popularity has waned because most species of turtle are now endangered and it's illegal to hunt them. Also, perhaps it's because there are fewer servants to do the difficult preparation. The recipe for the real thing is offered out of academic interest, only. It has been replaced on most menus by mock turtle soup, which has a similar gelatinous consistency and does not contain an endangered species as an ingredient.

a sea turtle

at least 1 veal knuckle

a couple of old hens

calves' feet

soup vegetables

basil

sage

sweet marjoram

savory

1 cup Madeira

pepper to taste

Thoroughly bleed the turtle, remove the meat from its shell, cut into small pieces, cook it in boiling salted water for 3 to 4 hours. Next, add the veal knuckle, the old hens, and as many calves' feet as are available. Cook for several more hours. Strain. Add the soup vegetables, cut up, for the last half hour of cooking. When ready to serve, add a pinch of each of the herbs, the Madeira, and the pepper. You may return the cooked meat to the broth or serve the clear soup.

MOCK TURTLE SOUP

Mock turtle soup is made by substituting the turtle, old hens and calves' feet in the above recipe with a calves' head, and cutting the cooking time in half.

MIDWEST TOMATOES STUFFED WITH CORN

6   tomatoes

2   ears corn (3 if the tomatoes are large)

2   tablespoons chopped onion

2   tablespoons chopped parsley

½   teaspoon salt

           pepper to taste

           butter

Slice the tops off the tomatoes, scoop out the pulp, and chop the pulp coarsely.
A grapefruit knife works well for this. Cut the corn from the cob with a sharp
knife. Combine pulp, corn, onions parsley and salt and pepper and fill the
tomato cups with the mixture; dot the top of each with butter. Place in a buttered baking pan, cover, and bake at 325 degrees F. for about 45 minutes, or
until the tomatoes are cooked through.

SONS AND LOVERS

by
D.H. Lawrence

"...as her sons grow up, she selects them as lovers—first the eldest, then the second," writes D.H. Lawrence to a friend as he describes a work in progress. The work is his powerful novel *Sons and Lovers*, whose characters unfold the œdipal complex with symbolic gestures and unknowing touches. Gertrude Morel sublimates sexual passion for her sons into a craving for their social and financial betterment. As well as encouraging them in their studies and instructing them in religious doctrine, their mother keeps a poor but genteel home, offering it as a love-token to her children.

As a young woman, this proud daughter of the lower-middle class loses her first love—an educated but weak-willed man—to a woman of property. Instead, she marries Walter Morel, not religious nor by any means intellectual, as she is considered to be, but intensely physical. At first she finds pleasure in his warm humor and in his vigorous young body and the joy he takes in it. Gertrude's father had been a solemn, proud and stern man. He was a high-minded Puritan, who eschewed pleasure and bitterly resented his poverty. It is no wonder, then, that the jovial and sensuous Morel held such a fascination for her. Gertrude and Walter, however, are married only a short time when she finds that he has deceived her, not only about the amount of his property, but also about the amount of his drinking. Their marriage bed is scarcely cold when fascination begins, slowly but relentlessly, to turn to revulsion. What had once seemed to be merriment in his nature becomes vulgarity, and finally, doused with more and more drink, obscenity. Bereft of refinement and sensitivity in her relationship with her husband, Gertrude Morel replaces him with her sons in her affections.

William, her eldest, is vibrant, strong, and prone to mischief. Fired by his mother's love, he is an accomplished athlete and wins prizes for running. The outgoing adolescent enjoys all the town can offer, "…from sixpenny hops down Church Street," to dancing with the sons and daughters of Bestwood's best. Steered by his mother into a career in business, William grows into a fiery, strapping stenographer, the second-best bookkeeper "on the place," and eventually takes a position with a London firm. Possessive and jealous, his mother disapproves of the attractive girls he meets at the local dances almost as much as she disapproves of his dancing, yet her stern puritanical demeanor hides a secret sensuality. As a young bride, she thrilled to her husband's virile body and physical nature. Now, no longer able to take pleasure in giving her body to her husband, she lays at her son's feet a voluptuous display of sweets; his favorite rice cake, mince pies, plum cake and an array of jewel-like tarts and cheesecakes await him on his first trip home from London.

Gertrude Morel's relationship with her second son, Paul, is the focal point of the novel, however, and he is also embraced with the fruits of her kitchen. Their bond is very close, and he responds to her love gestures of currant tarts and sweet delights by sharing in their creation. During his childhood, Paul and his mother are inseparable. Like D.H. Lawrence himself, purportedly a superb cook who often joined in the kitchen chores as a child, Paul Morel works side by side with his mother. He is never happier than when he shares the kitchen with her, whether briskly whipping egg whites or curled up on her chintz cushions, listening to the snapping fire and the rhythm of her devoted hands.

Paul is a sensitive child, disposed to mysterious fits of depression even as a toddler. He excels at painting, and his mother has great hopes for him as an artist. Her education to finer tastes lost in her marriage to a vulgar and self-satisfied miner, Gertrude Morel turns to Paul for the sensitivity she misses in her marriage. They share a love of beauty and order, managing, even in the grit and poverty of an English mining town, to find aesthetic sustenance. In a memorable scene, they admire a newly purchased little dish decorated with cornflowers, and imagine it filled with stewed fruit, a custard, or jelly.

Paul often helps with the bread baking, and it is during one of the regular Friday night baking sessions that a burned loaf sparks a quarrel between Paul and his mother. In perhaps the most dramatic scene of the novel, Mrs. Morel, in a jealous rage, accuses Paul of shifting his emotional loyalties to a neighbor girl, with whom she fears he is falling in love. It is only in this scene that Paul and his mother let down their guard of mother-son love, and even then they seem unaware of their feelings. After a round of furious accusations and guilty denials, mother and son embrace in conciliation.

"I've never—had a husband—not really—" He stroked his mother's hair, and his mouth was on her throat. "And she exults so in taking you from me—she's not like ordinary girls"

"Well, I don't love her, mother", he murmured, bowing his head and hiding his eyes on her shoulder in misery. His mother kissed him a long and fervent kiss.

"My boy!" she said, in a voice trembling with passionate love. Without knowing, he gently stroked her face.

Her jealous outburst to Paul is a rare one, for Mrs. Morel takes pride in her puritanical self-control. Neither she nor Paul seems conscious of the sexual implications of her powerful mother-love. To the boy, she is a tender and compassionate nurturer, ever-present with a cheering fire, a warm dinner, chintz cushions, and a perfectly kept house. Gertrude Morel steals the passion that belongs to her husband and gives it to her sons. They accept her molding of their lives, sustaining themselves on her carefully and lovingly prepared breads and puddings. Her gifts are joyously devoured by them, while no one in this family romance seems aware of the true significance of her culinary offerings.

000

Love treats from Gertrude Morel's pantry:

RICE CAKE

This cake has a luxuriously smooth texture and a delicate flavor, with only three ingredients. The secret is mixing until the batter is as light as air. That and eggs are the only leavening.

1 ½   cups rice flour (available in Asian markets.)

2   cups white sugar

5   whole eggs

Preheat oven to 325 degrees F.

Mix together the flour and sugar. In a separate bowl, beat the eggs well. Sift the dry ingredients into the eggs, and beat with an electric mixer on low speed for 20 minutes. Pour the batter into a buttered and floured tube pan and bake at 325 degrees for 35 minutes. Remove from the oven and cool upside down for 1-1/2 hours.

JAM TARTS

As far from the pre-fab version of this pastry commonly found in British luncheonettes as madeleines are from Twinkies, jam tarts are very simple to prepare. Just fit your favorite pie crust dough into small tart pans or muffin tins; then bake and cool. Melt any tart jam or preserves, and pour into ready shells. Boysenberry preserves makes an especially good filling. When the tarts are cooled and set, serve with whipped cream.

CURRANT TARTS

2   eggs

2/3   cup sugar

¼   teaspoon cinnamon

¼   teaspoon ground nutmeg

1 ½	teaspoon lemon juice
2	tablespoons melted butter
2/3	cup dried currants
¼	cup broken walnuts

Your favorite pastry dough

Line 4 large individual tart pans or 8 muffin tins with the pastry. Combine all the other ingredients and mix well, stirring in the currants and walnuts last. Pour into the unbaked tart shells, and bake 30 minutes at 375 degrees.

CHEESECAKES

What Mrs. Morel calls "cheesecake" is actually a tartlet made from cottage cheese, very popular in the English countryside at the time **Sons and Lovers** *was written. They are light, delicious, and unbelievably easy to make.*

your favorite pastry dough (enough to line 4 large or 6 small individual tart pans)

1	cup cottage cheese
½	cup sugar
3	egg yolks
4	tablespoons butter
1	teaspoon lemon juice

dash of nutmeg

Line 4 large or 6 small individual tart pans with the pastry. Combine the other ingredients in a blender and blend until smooth and creamy. Pour immediately into prepared pans, and bake at 350 degrees for 30 minutes.

TESS OF THE D'URBERVILLES

by
Thomas Hardy

Thomas Hardy's *Tess of the D'Urbervilles* opens with a May Day dance, a dance whose origins lie in the remote past of Druidic England. The women are dressed in white, carrying the ritual peeled willow branches and spring flowers, their long hair undulating in the sunlight. They dance with one another until the village laborers finish their day's work and join them in this ancient celebration of spring.

Wessex, as Hardy called the North Dorset Downs, is a stretch of land between the ancient temple of Stonehenge and the rustic Valley of the Little Dairies at Blackmoor Vale. It teems with symbols of fructifying nature: the pure beauty of young women, spring and renewal, birth and death. None of the old family estates there survived the Norman Conquest, and Wessex is populated primarily with agricultural laborers who owe their subsistence to their own independent labor. The area is alternately lush with vegetation and stark with fields of nothing but sand, gravel, and clay.

Tess of the D'Urbervilles begins in the north of Wessex, in the town of Marlott, located in the Valley of the Little Dairies. There are two classes of people in this tiny village—those who work hard and can afford to take their pleasure at the Pure Drop Inn, the better of the two drinking establishments in this one-and-a-half-pub town, and those on the other end of this broken village, those citizens who are less willing or less able to maintain a steady income—who gather at Rolliver's, a mere plank fastened to a garden fence that creates the facsimile of a bar. But Rolliver's also has a secret, dusty hide-away inside the owner's cottage, where the poor can "expand their souls" late into the night. Not fully licensed, the landlady invites "a few private friends" to join her behind the shawl-covered windows where, lost in the mists of her best quality drink, they perch upon the furniture and bask in the warmth of good fellowship and forgotten chores.

The villagers who frequent Rolliver's have too many children, eat what they can glean from the leavings of their labors, and finish the Monday wash by Friday if their luck holds. Pea soup, chitterlings, and other organ meat cost little, either in coins or advance planning. Marlott is largely inhabited by the uneducated, the superstitious, and the unreflective.

On a particularly cheerful evening at Rolliver's just after the May Day dance, the talk is of John Durbeyfield's recent news that he is related to the ancient and noble house of D'Uberville, one of the great families of Wessex, but thought to have been, like the others, extinct for many years. The news has transformed John Durbeyfield's life. Told by his doctor that although he is only in middle age, his heart is encased in a thick layer of fat (as Durbeyfield's wife describes it, "like a dripping pan"), and now learning that he has high-born ancestors, Durbeyfield lays down his minimal labors completely, believing himself now not only physically unfit to work, but functioning beneath his station socially as well. He sets to dreaming of lamb's fry for dinner instead of the usual chitterlings. He insists on traveling to and from Rolliver's by carriage, as befits his new status.

As a result of his increased social stature and decreased funds, Durbeyfield and his wife begin to look to their oldest daughter, Tess, as a possible means of support, thinking such a beauty a likely candidate for a successful match with one of the Stoke-D'Ubervilles, a prosperous family that owns a farm nearby. John and his wife, not realizing that the Stoke-D'Urbervilles are themselves only pretenders to the name, having adopted it because no one else was using it, decide to send Tess to "claim kin." Tess's mother dresses her daughter in the white gown of the May Day dance and sends her off to the waiting clutches of the moustachioed brute who will claim Tess's virtue, drive her to the ultimate crime of murder, thus perhaps even wrest from her eternal salvation. The childlike Mrs. Durbeyfield briefly considers the wisdom of their decision to send Tess away with the cynical remark "…if he don't marry her afore, he will after."

Desperate to help feed her foolish parents and her hungry siblings, Tess is finally seduced by her would-be cousin, who buys her compliance with gifts to the indigent Durbeyfields, but she leaves her hated lover to bear his child in secret, a weak and sickly baby who dies shortly after birth. Later, attempting to start over, Tess takes a job in "the Valley of the Great Dairies," where she spends some of her happiest days.

Tess's first view of her new home is of "…myriads of cows…outnumber[ing] any she had ever seen at one glance before…The ripe hue of the red and dun kine absorbed in the evening sunlight, which the white-coated animals returned to the eye in rays almost dazzling…" The water of the river was "clear as the pure River of Life shown to the Evangelist, rapid as the shadow of a cloud, with pebbly shallows that prattled to the sky…"

Life in the dairies is clean, orderly, and all of a piece. The regularity of the milking times, necessary to the quality of the butter and cream, divides the day into discreet portions, each with its particular character—a world away from the dishevelment and disorder of Tess's home at Marlott with her inebriate and daydreaming parents and their chaotic lives.

Tess quickly becomes a part of the life at the dairy farm, rising in the middle of the night with the others for the first milking, sleeping with her sister dairymaids above the milk-house. Her sleep at the end of a long day's labor mingles with the smell of cheeses and the sound of the dripping whey. Tess joins the others at the congenial dining-kitchen, the dairyman's wife presiding with home-made black puddings and mead. Out of this wholesome life, Tess rises like a fertility goddess, her gleaming hair, creamy skin, and rose-red mouth seeming to hold the secret and the promise of the May Day dance. To Angel Clare, the dairyman's pupil, Tess is not just a dairymaid "…but a visionary essence of woman."

But this seeming Garden of Eden is flawed, for on a walk one summer evening in June, Tess finds herself in an uncultivated part of the garden, "damp and rank with juicy grass…and tall blooming weeds," a dazzling polychrome of red, yellow, and purple. The weeds emit "offensive smells," and prick and stain her flesh. They seem to mock her hopes for a life of wholesomeness and order that the dairy represents and to hound her with the tidings that it is not possible to overcome the past. The growing love between Tess and Angel Clare will be haunted by the profanity of her first seduction.

000

LAMB'S FRY

John Durbeyfield's favorite dish, lamb's fry, is lamb testicles, breaded and sautéed. They are considered a delicacy in the western United States, where they are known as "Rocky Mountain oysters," due to their similarity in appearance to the shellfish. You will probably need to special order them from your butcher.

4	lamb testicles
1	slightly beaten egg mixed with a tablespoon of water
¾	cup dry bread crumbs
¼	cup butter for sautéing

Dip each testicle in the egg mixture, then dredge in the bread crumbs. Let them dry about 20 minutes before sautéing in melted butter until golden. Yield: 2 servings

FRIED CHITTERLINGS

Chitterlings ("chitlins" in the southern United States) are the small intestine of pigs, and are available in some meat markets.

5	pounds chitterlings
6	whole cloves
1	bay leaf
1	large onion, whole
1	celery stalk
1	teaspoon pepper
¼	cup vinegar
	boiling salted water
	flour
	butter

Cover the chitterlings with cold water and soak for 6 hours. Drain. Clean and wash. Bring the salted water to a boil and add the chitterlings with all the remaining ingredients except the flour and butter and simmer for 3 hours. Drain and cut into 2 inch pieces. Dip in flour and sauté in butter over medium heat until golden.

Yield: 4 servings

BLACK PUDDING

Black pudding, also known as blood pudding, is so called because of its color, and is actually a sausage. You will need fresh pork blood and sausage casings—the intestines of sheep, hogs, or cattle. Talk to your butcher about ordering both.

sausage casings

¾	cup finely chopped onions
½	lb. diced pork fat
2	cups fresh pig's blood
½	cup barley or rice
½	cup oatmeal
¼	teaspoon black pepper

Cook the barley or rice until soft. Mix the dry oatmeal with the pepper and a little of the blood to make a paste. Add the rice or barley, pork fat, onions pepper, and the remaining blood. Combine thoroughly. Fill the casings loosely with this mixture, twist at desired lengths, and tie with string to seal. Put the sausages into a wire basket and plunge them into boiling water. Reduce the heat and simmer for about 20 minutes. To serve, you may reheat in water, or grill.

TO THE LIGHTHOUSE

by
Virginia Woolf

But she stopped. There was a smell of burning. Could they have let the *boef en daube* overboil? She wondered, pray heaven not! when the great clangor of the gong announced solemnly, authoritatively, that all those scattered about, in attics, in bedrooms, on little perches of their own, reading, writing, putting the last smooth to their hair, or fastening dresses, must leave all that, and the little odds and ends of their washing-tables, and the diaries which were so private, and assemble in the dining-room for dinner.

After the above paragraph, in Virginia Woolf's *To the Lighthouse*, each guest at the Ramsay's summer house party leaves his reading, his toilet, his little perch, and takes a seat at the candle-studded table, where the various struggles of the diners: Minta's lost brooch, Mr. Tansley's dissertation on "the influence of something on something," and Lily Briscoe's painting are as much a part of the tableau their hostess creates as is the luscious yellow and purple centerpiece of fruits.

During the soup course, while she awaits the presentation of her esteemed *boef en daube*, Mrs. Ramsay mentally drifts from her dutiful hostess conversation about the welfare of lighthouse keepers to dinners of twenty years ago, when one moved about in drawing rooms "without haste or anxiety, for there was no future to worry about." Life, she reflects, "was sealed up there and lay, like a lake, placidly between its banks." She muses on a time when people were able to appreciate their present moments, and dining was a ritualistic observance of day's end. Personal struggles were set aside in favor of a peaceful gathering together in calm fellowship with one's guests.

In contrast to this graceful world of another time, life at Mrs. Ramsay's table "shoots down in cascades"; the tension of lost mementos, uncompleted work, and the thwarted wishes of her husband, who must suffer the delay of a guest appreciatively requesting seconds of soup, surround the placid hostess, and only she fully savors the moment. In this novel of artistic struggle, Mrs. Ramsay sees the world as a painter might. The candle-flames draw her guests into her range of vision, and they appear like seated diners in a painting. She lovingly regards the colors and shapes of the purple grapes and yellow pears and bananas which decorate the table, and visualizes Augustus, the soup-loving poet, as a foraging bee, landing here and there on sweet blossoms.

Where once there were separate individuals on separate "perches," reading, grooming or letter writing, Mrs. Ramsay perceives a composition of faces, united, by the table, the candles and the fruit, shut off from the wavering darkness of the night by the opaque windows, an island of "order and dry land," the outside, a "reflection in which things wavered and vanished..." Mrs. Ramsay's dinner is, as Robert Frost described the value of his own art, "a momentary stay against confusion."

Lily Briscoe's struggle to complete her painting, the central metaphor of the novel, echoes in Mrs. Ramsay's urge to unite the disconnected. As she serves the soup, she reflects that all her guests seem to sit separately up and down the two sides of the table, and it is up to her to bring them together on common ground. Given Mr. Ramsay's impulses, it is fitting that she should have chosen a stew, a dish in which many ingredients mingle to create a single effect instead of, say, a single piece of meat surrounded by satellites of vegetables and potatoes, each basking in its own identity instead of the shared identity that comes with the exchange of flavors and textures in a common pot. Mrs. Ramsay inhales the vapors of the *boef en daube* as she dips into her grandmother's treasured recipe, its "exquisite scent of olives and juice," and describes the contents of the pot as a painter might see it: "...its shiny walls and its confusion of savoury brown and yellow meats and its bay leaves and its wine..."

The table exudes a Rembrandt-like quality as the candles illuminate the earth-toned bounty. In their soft glow, the yellow pears and bananas resound in the golden color of the fatted pork and blend with the rich brown of the meat and its juices in the earthenware pot. Mrs. Ramsay notices the candle flames reflected in the blackness of the night windows and, mirror-like, the scene is duplicated within the frames.

Although the hostess artfully creates the scene, pulling together the elements of the party to create a single, unified effect, it is actually her cook who has prepared the meal. *The cook had spent three days over that dish*, thinks Mrs. Ramsay, as another servant ceremoniously removes the cover.

000

BOEUF en DAUBE

Few of us have the means to afford the cook and the table attendant, which allowed Mrs. Ramsay the luxury of a meditative mood at her own dinner party, yet in spite of its long simmering time, Boef en Daube is a surprisingly simple dish to prepare. Originally, it was allowed to stew slowly, buried in hot cinders and charcoal, and this may indeed have taken three days. Another less time-consuming way to prepare it, however, is to marinate the beef overnight before cooking. If you insist on three days to prepare your dish, just as Mrs. Ramsay's cook did, you can increase this step to two days without harm. Also, the dish is all the better for splitting the cooking time in half, over two days, three hours on each, letting the flavors mingle between sessions in the oven. Although the following recipe is a trifle more red than brown, you can use white wine and fresh tomatoes instead of red wine and tomato paste, but the result will not be as rich.

2 ½	lbs. beef chuck cut into 2 inch pieces
2	tablespoons olive oil
1	cup red wine
½	teaspoon thyme
2	bay leaves
1	onion, sliced
2	garlic cloves, minced
	black pepper to taste
1	6 ounce can of tomato paste
12	pimento stuffed olives
¼ lb.	ham, salt pork or bacon (The fatter the pork, the yellower the finished product, and thus the closer to Mrs. Ramsay's description. The leaner the pork, the cleaner your veins.)

Mix the olive oil, wine, pepper, thyme, bay leaves, garlic and onion in a large bowl. Place the beef in this mixture, cover and refrigerate overnight. Then put the beef, marinade, and all other ingredients in an earthenware pot. Cover and place in a 300 degree oven for six hours. Since the sauce is quite rich, serve with plain rice and a simple vegetable or salad.

WORKS CONSULTED

Ayrton, Elizabeth. *The Cookery of England*. London: Andre Deutch, 1975.

Beard, James. *American Cookery*. Boston: Little, Brown, 1972.

Beeton, Mrs. Isabella. *The Book of Household Management*. (facsimile) U.S.: Farrar, Straus & Giroux, 1969.

Bjornskov, Elizabeth. *The Complete Book of American Fish and Shellfish Cookery*. New York: Alfred A. Knopf, 1984.

Boyd, Lizzie. *British Cookery*. Woodstock, N. Y.: Overlook Press, 1979.

Goldstein, Darra. *À La Russe*. New York: Random House, 1983.

Hamman, Mary. ed. *Picture Cook Book*. New York: Time Incorporated, 1958.

Johnson, Ronald. *The American Table*. New York: William Morrow and Company, 1984.

Krohn, Norman Odya. *Menu Mystique*. New York: Jonathan David Publishers, 1983.

Montagné, Prosper. *Larousse Gastronomique*. New York: Crown Publishers, 1961.

Ortiz, Elizabeth Lambert. *The Book of Latin American Cooking*. New York: Alfred A. Knopf, 1979.

Perkins, Wilma Lord, (revisions). *The Fannie Farmer Cookbook*. Boston: Little, Brown, 1965.

Princess Pamela's Soul Food Cookbook. New York: New American Library, 1969.

Rombauer, Irma S. and Marion Rombauer Becker. *Joy of Cooking*. New York: Bobbs-Merrill, 1964.

Simon, André L. *A Concise Encyclopaedia of Gastronomy*. New York: Bramball House, 1939.

Stern, Jane and Michael. *American Gourmet*. New York: Harper Collins, 1992.

Winer, Bart, ed. Ph. Gilbert, et al. *The Art of French Cooking*. New York: Golden Press, 1962.

0-595-32951-9

CPSIA information can be obtained at www.ICGtesting.com
Printed in the USA
BVOW05s1116200414

351087BV00002B/160/A

9 780595 329519